How the message of *Fully Alive* is helping people all over the world . . .

"Larry's teaching on gender has impacted my personal life, my marriage, and my leadership of the men's ministry at my church. Moving forward into messy situations in faith rather than passively letting chaos reign has allowed me to see God work in new ways in my marriage and in ministry." —Charles B., Chicago, IL, husband/father/pastor

"Seeing the potential in giving and receiving, I realize it is a waste of time to compete. Both men and women will benefit greatly by honoring their calling, resulting in freedom and joy. In spite of my age, sixty-five years old, I feel challenged and excited." —Tom N., Stange, Norway, husband/father/retired

"*Feminine* and *woman* used to be words that dripped with connotations of weakness and vulnerability—an invitation to be used. Yet the essence of my feminine heart longed to be seen, cherished, honored, protected, and enjoyed. This heart of mine has begun to step out of the shadows and into the warm embrace of the True Light Himself. A deep joy has been released in me as I honor the dignity of my heart as a woman. I am more alive now than ever, and I bless God for that." —Kjersten H., Colorado Springs, CO, single/counselor

"Dr. Crabb's teaching on gender taught me a new way of relating to my wife. There is a drastic shift in my soul—my 'shrinking back' fear has been replaced by a 'standing tall' movement toward her. This new way has breathed life into our marriage." —John F., Greensboro, NC, husband/father/pastor

"Whether I am counseling a client or journeying through spiritual formation with a brother in Christ, Larry Crabb's teaching on gender roles continues to enlighten my discussions. I experienced a distinct paradigm shift in my counseling upon learning about how gender relates to being created in God's image. Now there is an increasing desire to live out His strength in being the man He created me to be." —David W., Burleson, TX, husband/father/counseling pastor

"I had just come out of divorce from an abusive thirty-year marriage when I heard Larry teach on masculinity and femininity. The Lord used that teaching to begin the restoration process of my shattered soul and identity of who God created me to be. I am an image bearer, and as a woman I am called to openly and courageously invite others to be consumed by God's love." —Kerry F., Scottsdale, AZ, single/counselor

"Both of us have been through Larry's School of Spiritual Direction, and it was one of the most impactful weeks of our lives. His gender message is biblically based and easy to understand. It has revolutionized the way we relate to each other. We believe this book is vital for those desiring authentic marital intimacy." —Ryan and Heather C., Forest, VA, husband/pastoral counselor and wife/mentor

"Dr. Crabb's teaching on gender has been the best source for understanding femininity and masculinity that I have found. There is something beautiful and inviting about me as a woman that has nothing to do with my appearance. I love knowing that truth and its biblical foundation. It has impacted the way I view myself as well as how I view men. I hope more people hear it and that we might all be set free to be the men and women God designed us to be." —Mary Beth M., Austin, TX, single/spiritual mentor/film producer

"The shackles of fear, shame, and confusion have been broken down. Larry's insightful biblical teaching on masculinity and femininity have freed men and women from the bondage placed on them by religion and society. We are now free to 'move toward' and 'open up' to one another in love to reveal the unconditional love of the Trinity." —Jason D., Fort Hood, TX, husband/father/military chaplain

"This teaching has caused a revolutionary shift in my paradigm of womanhood that is reflected in how I relate to my spouse, my children, my friends, and the world. It forever changes how I am, uniquely as a woman, to reflect the Trinity. Everyone should read this book. It changes everything." —Jeanne M. Frankenmuth, MI, pastor's wife/mother

"I've struggled my whole life with a debilitating fear of criticism and the need to have the approval of others. Larry's teaching has helped me realize I've had a false definition of what it means to be a man. I'm amazed at how much impact this has had on the quality of my relationships now that I've stopped hiding." —Jon L., Omaha, NE, husband/father/minister

"I wasn't able to see myself as a woman the way God created me to be, because I wasn't married yet. I didn't understand what biblical femininity was all about. Through Larry's teaching, I saw for the first time how God created me as a woman who could glorify Him through my femininity, whether married or single. My view about that and myself has changed, and I am now free to be a woman for God's glory." —Natalia M., Moldova, single/missionary

"Larry's insight into how God has uniquely created men and women to engage and reflect God to one another has been a challenge and a blessing. Especially in the lives of my clients, the 'light switch' turns on that there is more than just the 'roles' that society and the church have established. God has ordained and created a beautiful dance between husband and wife that only the music of heaven can lead." —Greg C., Houston, TX, husband/father/counselor

"Hearing Larry explain and express the core terrors of men and women and having accurate biblical definitions of what it is to be male or female has led me to profound longing for the weight of God—His *kabod*—in my life and joy when, in passing moments, I am aware of being a truly alive man." —Graham B., Aberdeen, Scotland, husband/father/pastor

FULLY
ALIVE

FULLY ALIVE

A Biblical Vision of Gender That
Frees Men and Women
to Live Beyond Stereotypes

DR. LARRY CRABB

BakerBooks
a division of Baker Publishing Group
Grand Rapids, Michigan

© 2013 by Larry Crabb

Published by Baker Books
a division of Baker Publishing Group
P.O. Box 6287, Grand Rapids, MI 49516-6287
www.bakerbooks.com

Paperback edition published 2014
ISBN 978-0-8010-1533-5

Printed in the United States of America

The Library of Congress has cataloged the hardcover edition as follows:
Crabb, Lawrence J.
    Fully alive : a Biblical vision of gender that frees men and women to live beyond stereotypes
/ Dr. Larry Crabb.
      pages cm
    ISBN 978-0-8010-1530-4 (cloth)
    ISBN 978-0-8010-1592-2 (pbk.)
    1. Sex role—Religious aspects—Christianity. I. Title.
BT708.C73 2013
261.8′357—dc23   2012049936

To protect the privacy of those who have shared their stories with the author, some details and names have been changed.

In keeping with biblical principles of creation stewardship, Baker Publishing Group advocates the responsible use of our natural resources. As a member of the Green Press Initiative, our company uses recycled paper when possible. The text paper of this book is composed in part of post-consumer waste.

15 16 17 18 19 20   7 6 5 4 3 2

To Rachael,
A God-revealing woman

A student from twenty years ago reminded me
of something I said in class when I was in my forties.
I remember saying it:
"I wonder what book I'll write when I care more about
what God thinks than what people think."

This may be that book, perhaps the first of many.

Contents

PROLOGUE

I never heard my mother pray. She never told me Bible stories when I was a child or sang Sunday school choruses to me. Mother knew God, and she knew Jesus as her Savior, but steeping me in Christianity was my father's job. He was a man. She was a woman. Her job, as was true of all godly women, was to fade into the domestic background; to help, never lead; to support, never teach. That was how we thought in our church circles. At the time, I had no idea that such thinking was widespread in culture.

Mother was both a bright and beautiful woman. A university-trained occupational therapist, for years she managed the occupational therapy program at a private psychiatric hospital. I've seen pictures of her when she was a young bride. By my culture's standard, she was more than attractively feminine. She wore dresses, kept her figure, had a pretty face, and looked after her family.

Seven mornings and seven evenings each week, with few exceptions, mother cooked breakfast and dinner. She filled her cracks of time with cleaning, washing clothes, carting me to the doctor and dentist as needed, grocery shopping, and laying a cool cloth on my forehead when I was burning with fever. She was a woman. That's what women did.

In the third year of her seven-year descent into Alzheimer's that ended her life at age eighty-seven, in a rare unguarded and spontaneous moment, Mother put words to an unbearable agony that I now think had lain dormant within her since girlhood. As I was leading her to my car for a lunch outing, with Dad walking slowly behind, Mother suddenly stopped, and with terrified eyes looking into mine, tearfully said, "I'm no good to anyone."

That was only the second time I had ever seen my mother cry. The first time, many decades earlier, came about when I, as an eight-year-old bratty child who had not gotten his way, petulantly—no, cruelly—told Mother how mean she was, that she was the worst mother in the world. I shouldn't have been, but I was startled when she cried. I remember being stunned by the instant realization, *She's not just my mom, she's a woman.* I immediately backpedaled and tearfully told her I didn't mean what I had just said, that she was really a wonderful mother, anything to get her to stop crying. I couldn't bear to see her in pain.

She died several years ago. I'm left wondering, *Did my mother ever feel she was deeply good to anyone, that her life brought rich pleasure to God, to her family, to others, to anybody?*

I think not, and this realization pains me today: what could have been, but wasn't. I'm grateful to be her son. According to her understanding of what God designed a woman to be and to do, she was a good woman, a faithful wife, a well-intentioned mother who expressed love in deeds, not words. I never remember her telling me that she loved me.

Although that non-memory is sad, my saddest thought now is that perhaps my mother never knew, never even asked herself, *What would it mean to be fully alive as an image-bearing female in whatever relationships my life provides, and in whatever opportunities to advance God's kingdom come my way that I am called and gifted to seize?* Had she asked that question and freely decided that her calling and gifting were most fully expressed in domestic opportunities, my mother would have found meaning and joy in all the good things she did for our family.

My father's story is different, but disturbingly similar. I often heard my father pray. I first believed that there was a God as I listened to my father pray one Sunday morning in church when I was five years old. Sixty people, including children, gathered in a large circle every Sunday morning to remember the Lord in His death. By that time, I had heard many men pray in my few years. Women, of course, were not permitted to pray aloud. We were taught they were to keep silent in the church.

The men's prayers always seemed formal and predictable. I once timed Bill Nelson's prayer—twenty-four minutes. But that one Sunday morning, as he often had before, my father stood to pray. I was lying on the carpeted floor of our church building, hoping Mr. Nelson wouldn't pray again. I don't know why—I suppose it had something to do with God's Spirit—but I looked up at Dad when he began to pray. And it struck me: *he thinks he's talking to somebody!* Within seconds, I sat up and nearly said out loud: "Ohmigosh. He's talking to God!" At that moment I became a convinced theist. Three years later I became a believing Christian.

Dad loved the Bible. When I was twelve, he was telling me about Jesus opening up the Old Testament to show the Christ to two despairing disciples walking on the road to Emmaus. I remember him pausing, looking away from me (I think now he was fixing his eyes on the real but invisible world), and with an almost childish excitement and awe, shuddering as he spoke, he said these exact words: "Wouldn't it be something to be in a Bible study with the Author?"

Dad's father died when he was only five. After completing eighth grade, Dad dropped out of school to get a job to help support his widowed mother and three siblings. In his twenties he landed a sales job with a large corporation that carried a salary sufficient to free him to propose to my mother. A few years later, his superior insisted he follow company custom and provide women to sleep with valued customers.

In the spirit of Joseph, my father replied, "No. I cannot offend my Lord in this way." He lost his job. A promising career ended. Dad then began a small business that for years required long hours and brought in uncertain money. With Mother's help, Dad kept my brother and me fed, clothed, and relatively comfortable.

Looking back, I gratefully realize that Dad fathered us well: my brother, Bill, through his long rebellion, and me through my faith struggles during my graduate school days in psychology. And I have no doubt that he deeply loved my mother.

But I do not believe it ever occurred to him to move as a man toward my mother in ways intended to release her to come fully alive as a woman. Instead, I think he celebrated mother's conformity to their mostly undiscussed but agreed-upon vision that centered on "the role of women" as submissively helpful and unaggressively supportive. I may have missed it, but through five decades of knowing my parents I never saw Dad looking at Mother with eyes that wondered, *Who is this remarkable woman? What can I do, who can I be, that would encourage her to freely give everything within her for God's kingdom, for God's glory, for her joy, for the blessing of others?*

I don't think he resisted that thought. I think it never occurred to him. And I'm not sure he thought about what he could do as a man to deepen his two sons in their masculinity. He fervently wanted Bill and me to love God and others, but as Christians, not so much as Christian men.

In his post-seventy years, Dad often expressed to me how small he felt, how useless and insignificant, how he wondered why God was keeping him alive on earth. I asked myself then, and I ask myself even more now, *Did my father ever enjoy his deepest calling as a man, a calling that could have continued through his senior years until the moment of death?*

I think not. I don't believe my father ever knew, or knew to ask, what it would mean to be fully alive as an image-bearing male.

Irenaeus, an early church father, once famously wrote, "The glory of God is a human being made fully alive." Let me reshape that thought a bit, and re-state it as the question that incited me to write this book:

What does it mean to be fully alive as a male or female for the glory of God?

I don't want our two sons, now middle-aged men, to lament a few decades from now that their mother and I never seriously and with joy asked that question. I want our sons, our two daughters-in-law, and our five grandchildren to celebrate their femininity or masculinity as God-designed opportunities to bring God's rule to earth. I want them to do so by revealing through the way they relate something wonderful about the way God relates, both within His own eternal community of Three Persons and with us, His beloved children.

And I want the same for you, my readers, men and women who were born as male or female, part of a divine plan that brings with it the joyful sense of purpose that God wants you to know in all your relationships, even the difficult ones.

As you prepare to read this book, let me suggest that you entertain some questions I don't think my mother and dad ever asked. They are questions rarely asked today in our churches, families, or friendships. But they are questions that must be asked if we're to fulfill God's design for our lives. After all, we were created male and female.

- What did God have in mind when He created us as male or female? Only pleasurable procreation? Only happy marriages? Is there anything else He had in mind? Perhaps more? Something more transcendent that everyone—married or single—can enjoy?
- What does it mean to be fully alive for God's glory as a male or female? Are you fully alive in your maleness or femaleness?
- What makes a woman *deeply feminine* in a way that reveals something wonderfully unique about how God relates? Is that a new question? Does it intrigue you? Do you, a woman, see yourself as feminine? When? Why?
- What makes a man *deeply masculine* in a way that reveals something wonderfully unique about how God relates? Is that a new question? Does it intrigue you? Do you, a man, see yourself as masculine? When? Why?
- Do we fall short of revealing God's character by failing to relate as feminine women and masculine men? Have we understood sin to include *relational* sin? Or do we consider sin to be little more than obviously bad behavior?
- What does it mean for a single woman to be fully alive in her femininity? What does it mean for a single man to be fully alive in his masculinity? Is it possible? Can a single person be as fully feminine or masculine as a married person? Might singleness be a unique opportunity to seize, for God's purposes, a calling at least as high as marriage?
- Could there be a relationship between the failure to relate as masculine men and feminine women and same-sex attractions, promiscuity, sexual addictions, or sexual fears?
- Can we understand the rule of God, the coming of Christ's kingdom to earth, to centrally involve the development of a kind of community that only develops among feminine women and masculine men as they live out their gender in how they relate? Stanley Grenz put it this way: "When God's rule is present—when God's will is done—community emerges."[1] What does he mean? Is he right?

Big questions. Lots of questions. Questions that are not often asked or easily answered. But they are important for everyone who longs to know the meaning, hope, and joy of living as we were meant to live—as gendered bearers of God's image.

1. Stanley J. Grenz, *Theology for the Community of God* (Eerdmans: Grand Rapids, 2000), 24.

My parents lived in a way that brought God pleasure. They enjoyed a good marriage. But how much more of God's relational beauty could they have revealed to me, and how much more of their gendered nature could they have enjoyed, had they asked these questions and searched for answers in the Bible?

To my parents—to their memory that lives in me and to their sense of completion as male and female that they now and forever fully enjoy—I am indebted, and with warm appreciation dedicate this book.

Acknowledgments

Thanks to the Baker Books team who, from our first breakfast meeting in Denver, had a vision for this project and devoted their considerable talents and energy to help make it all it could be throughout its development. Chad, Mike, Lindsey, and the rest of the team—you've been great to work with.

Thanks to all the students in our School of Spiritual Direction for journeying with me as my thoughts on gender took shape. You've helped me realize that God's vision of gender reaches deep into the human soul with liberating power.

Thanks to Tom and Jenny, and Bob and Claudia. Rachael and I have been walking together with you for nearly a decade in our intentional spiritual formation group, each of us longing to become more of whom God designed us to be as men and women. It's a *good* journey.

Thanks to Andi: colleague, friend, and sister. I can't imagine doing what I do without you. Your excitement about my "gender stuff" encouraged me to write this book.

Thanks to my two sons: to Ken, whose discerning interest in this project and whose dozens of thoughtful conversations did more to keep me going than you realize, and to Kep, whose book-agenting guided the process of moving thoughts into book form and whose wise feedback as you typed the manuscript is visible in each chapter.

And to Rachael, my wife of nearly fifty years, the woman I know best and appreciate most. Honey, you live femininity in ways that arouse me to become the masculine man I was created to be. I've said it a million times and I'll say it a million times more: I love you!

INTRODUCTION

Think of a marriage, a family, a friendship, a small group of missionaries serving in a foreign country, a church gathering, an elder board, colleagues at work, or golfing buddies . . .

Wherever people have the opportunity to meet.

Now picture a bridge, a narrow bridge, stretching over a deep chasm.

One person stands at one end of the bridge, a second person stands at the other end. The two people are facing each other. They can see each other's expressions. They can hear each other's voices. But they never connect.

Picture the people as two women. Or two men. Or one man and one woman. It doesn't matter. The one constant is obvious: there is distance between them, whatever their gender. They do not meet on the bridge.

And yet the sign on each end of the bridge says: "The Bridge of Connection." This bridge provides the opportunity for two women, two men, or one man and one woman to meet. It's what they want to do:

- The two women want to connect as sisters or as friends.
- The two men want to connect as brothers or as friends.
- The man and woman want to connect as brother and sister or perhaps as lovers.

They were designed to connect, to meet at a level that deeply satisfies their longing hearts. But they never really meet. It never happens.

What will it take:

- for two women to meet as fully alive women?
- for two men to meet as fully alive men?

- for a man and a woman to meet as a fully alive man and a fully alive woman, as brother and sister or as long-term lovers who will love each other with God-like love forever?

This book draws from the wisdom of the community where *connecting* is defined—the Trinity of the Father, Son, and Holy Spirit—to suggest how men and women can meet and relate on the Bridge of Connection.

PART I

SEARCHING FOR OUR GENDERED CENTER

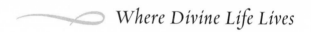 *Where Divine Life Lives*

We cannot say that humanity is divided into the "sanguine" and the "cho-leric" temperaments, into extraverts and introverts, into white and coloured races, into geniuses and non-geniuses, but humanity certainly is divided into men and women, and this distinction goes down to the very roots of our personal existence, and penetrates into the deepest "metaphysical" grounds of our personality and destiny.

Emil Brunner[1]

At the core of who we are, we are gendered. Femininity or masculinity is so irrevocably and irreversibly embedded in our being that no one can accurately say, "I am first a person and then male or female." With the

---

1. Emil Brunner, *Man in Revolt*, trans. Olive Wyon (Philadelphia: Westminster Press, 1939), 345.

privileged excitement of destiny, we must rather say, "I am a male person, a man," or "I am a female person, a woman." Our soul's center is alive with either masculinity or femininity. Our uniquely gendered style of relating is clearly visible in our interactions when it reflects something wonderful about the relational nature of our beyond-gender God.

And so we must ask, "What makes a man masculine? What makes a woman feminine?"

1

SEX AND GENDER

When we know God well enough to value nothing greater than our opportunity to enjoy Him and reveal Him to others by the way we relate, we will then become more and more alive as masculine men and feminine women.

We must begin with the most basic question: What's the difference between sex and gender? Recognizing the sex of the child—whether a newborn infant is male or female is (usually) relatively easy. Genitalia tells the story. With confidence that requires no medical training, the doctor informs the parents, "It's a boy!" or "It's a girl!" The parents then take it from there. They name and dress the child accordingly. Most Christians agree that God made males to be men and females to be women, and because of God's design, anatomically determined sex is intended to express itself in socially identified gender.

But not always. I recently read the account of a baby born in Sweden. When the parents were asked by friends, "Is it a boy or a girl?" they calmly answered, "Our child will decide that later. Our child will eventually let us know whether we have a son or daughter."

In rare cases of hermaphroditism, babies are born with both male and female genitalia. A decision usually follows. Doctors can implement the decision by surgically forming the child as a male or female. In later years, that child might wonder why he feels like a girl trapped in a boy's body or why she feels like a boy trapped in a girl's body. In our fallen existence, complications sometimes arise that seem unanswerable and difficult, if not impossible, to unravel.

The article I read made no mention that the Swedish baby was born with both sexual organs, so I assumed the child's biological *sex* was not in question. But in the parents' thinking, the child's *gender* was up for grabs. In their minds, the child's sex did not determine gender. The decision to adopt the social identity of a boy or girl was left to the child. Someone had to make the decision; why not let it be made by the one who would have to live with it?

The parents therefore clothed their child in a pretty dress one day and little boy's trousers the next. Their plan was to continue that pattern until the child seemed more drawn toward one gender or the other.

Their thinking is clear: *sex and gender are separable*. Sex, whether a child is male or female, is fixed (in most cases) at birth. Anatomy makes that decision. But gender, whether a child will live as a boy or girl and eventually a man or woman, is a personal decision. Chosen gender need not correspond to anatomical sex.

An American educator took this idea a big step further. I watched a video clip of a man passionately telling a classroom full of elementary school children that one's gender was not only a choice, it was a flexible choice. If a boy wanted to live permanently as a girl or if a girl wanted to live permanently as a boy, sexual reassignment by surgery was certainly an option. One's chosen gender could then match one's physical sex. But our personal freedom, said the teacher, is greater than a one-time choice to switch genders. Let sex—the anatomy—remain fixed, but choose gender at will.

If I heard him correctly, the teacher was implying that without altering one's anatomy, any person can choose to be a boy today, a girl tomorrow; a young woman in college, a man throughout adulthood; and in their senior years, an old lady or an old man. Never feel limited by your body. Gender is always a choice.

Neither the Swedish parents' view nor the American educator's teaching represents mainstream culture—not yet, anyway. But without surrendering to what most Christians agree is the biblical revelation that God made males to be men and females to be women, without a corresponding belief that by God's design anatomically determined sex is intended to express itself in socially identified gender, ideas that sound extreme today could become mainstream tomorrow.

The Starting Point

Our culture is sexually confused. And at the center of our confusion is the absence of a well-thought-out agreement about what makes a male person a masculine man and about what makes a female person a feminine woman. Reaching agreement on such a controversy-riddled issue requires an agreed-upon starting point.

Most evangelicals, I think, believe that when God made us male and female human beings, He intended that our *gender*, our social identity as masculine men and feminine women, would correspond to our *sex*, our physical makeup as males or females. If you were born a male, you live as a man, look like a man, and relate to others as a man. If you were born a female, you live as a woman, look like a woman, and relate to others as a woman.

That starting point, however, immediately raises difficult questions. What does it mean to live, look, and relate as men and women, to be *masculine* or *feminine*? The very words *masculinity* and *femininity* fill our minds with silly images, superficial cultural stereotypes left over from earlier eras that continue to haunt us today: three-piece suits and frilly blouses, tough guys and tender women, broad shoulders and shapely legs, absent fathers who work hard and present mothers who cook well, strong male leaders and submissive female followers.

If we leave these stereotypes behind, then another question needs to be asked: Do Christians have any biblical basis that we can draw from to understand what it really means for males and females to become masculine men and feminine women? Because we bear God's image, can men and women reveal something uniquely wonderful about God by the way we relate? Is that question even important?

The church's response to our culture's sex and gender confusion seems inadequate to me. We have so strongly focused on either the role of women or the equal rights of women that we have given little thought to *the unique relational opportunities* of men and women. Traditionalists believe they have biblical reason for keeping women "in their place." Egalitarians worry that a failure to emphasize equality over uniqueness might permit men to remain in "dominating leadership" in positions of authority (especially in the church).

Their worry is warranted. In my growing-up years, I often heard men in my church speak condescendingly about "the role of women." I never heard a man speak similarly about "the role of men." The message was implicit but clear: women are restricted, men are free. Leadership belongs to men, women quietly follow. My parents lived that message.

What I'm not hearing in our sex/gender debates today is a thoughtful, biblically dependent, open-minded discussion of what it means for men to resemble God in their masculinity and for women, with equal importance but uniquely and differently, to resemble God in their femininity.

Patriarchal traditionalists emphasize male leadership, if not in the working world, then certainly in the church and family. Hierarchical traditionalists insist on the flipside of the same coin: men's leadership requires women's subordination. Women enjoy equal value, perhaps, but not equal opportunity. Women must remain in their God-assigned place. That's what *feminine* women do.

Complementarians gladly acknowledge that men and women are different, and insist that the God-created differences lie mainly in gender-defined roles. Masculine men lead. Feminine women submit. Some complementarians veer further from traditionalists when they suggest that gender differences provide women with the opportunity to complement men by relating with feminine tenderness while men continue to lead with masculine strength. Final authority, though, remains with the man in both family and church.

Egalitarians often agree that men and women are different. But rather than exploring our gender uniqueness with the hope of releasing men and women into their God-designed masculinity and femininity, their focus centers on the full equality of women with men. Especially in marriage, but also in all relationships—social, ecclesial, or professional—men and women are to relate as equal partners, loving each other, respecting each other, honoring each other's differences, submitting to each other in healthy dialogue when opinions differ, and living with equal freedom to pursue every desired opportunity to exercise their gifts and to honor whatever their calling. Equal rights for women is their focus, not unique gendered opportunities.

What it means to live, look, and relate as men and women fully alive in their masculinity and femininity remains an inadequately explored question. With a freshness and zeal I did not anticipate, I'm now asking what makes a man masculine and what makes a woman feminine, and how differences in the way men and women were designed to relate, if indeed they exist, together reveal something about our relational God that He wants us to see and enjoy. I'm looking to the Bible to see if God has any thoughts on the matter.

New Question, New Thoughts

After thirty years as a clinical psychologist, practicing and teaching my understanding of Christian counseling, a deeper and more radical grasp of Christianity got the best of me. A question began to burn in my mind that I hadn't seriously asked before: *What does it mean to become fully alive in Christ by the Spirit for the Father's glory?*

We exist to tell God's story. God does not exist to tell ours. We're to become fully alive for God's sake, to glorify Him by enjoying Him and revealing Him to others. Living for any other purpose leads to death.

It is death. Whatever feeling of life it produces is an illusion.

It occurred to me the conversations that really mattered were conversations that somehow released more of Christ's life in a person's soul, empowering us to better tell God's story. And it slowly dawned on me that neither psychotherapy nor counseling, as practiced by secular professionals and as too commonly practiced by Christians, qualified by this criterion as conversations that mattered. They aimed too low, toward symptom relief and pleasant feelings, with methods more grounded in research than revelation. Spiritual direction, releasing Christ's life through Spirit-guided conversations into souls hungry to enjoy God and reveal God, became my consuming interest. Soon after, the School of Spiritual Direction was birthed.

For ten years now, four times a year, I've been leading a one-week program called the School of Spiritual Direction. For the first three years, I focused on coming alongside image-bearing persons to encourage the process of becoming spiritually formed, to become like Jesus as they followed Jesus. Then several more thoughts hit me. The first one was not new, but it came with new force: we bear the image of a relational God, the Trinity. To be truly formed like Jesus means to relate like Jesus. *Spiritual* formation is *relational* formation.

A second thought quickly followed: we are not only image-bearing persons, we are *gendered* image-bearing persons. Genesis 1:27 makes that clear. Now I had to ask what it meant to be relationally formed as gendered persons, to relate like Jesus as men and women. It was then that the words *masculinity* and *femininity* came alive with new meaning, a new meaning that I wanted to explore.

Could it be, I wondered, *that masculinity and femininity have something to do with how men and women relate in human community, how they relate by the Spirit's power in ways that correspond to how the Father and Son relate in divine community?*

A third thought then exploded in my mind. Could it be that we become answers to the Lord's prayer by bringing God's divine kingdom of relational community to earth through relating as masculine men and feminine women? Did God create us as image-bearing males and females so that men and women could each reveal, by the way we relate, something of the wonder of how the persons of the Trinity relate?

Hormones, genitals, and the distribution of XY chromosomes define a person's physical sex. Surgeons can go a long way, though not all the way, in changing someone's born sex. Clothing, hairstyle, and mannerisms give evidence of the social identity as male or female that someone has adopted, although in these unisex days the evidence is sometimes unclear.

Gender issues find their way to center stage when the *religious design* (gender roles as understood by the church) for men and women becomes the topic. The discussion is often heated. But neither anatomy nor appearance (except in fundamentalist cultures where women must wear knee-covering skirts or shape-hiding robes) is responsible for the heat. The battle is engaged over roles versus freedom—typically for women, not men. Depending on one's theology, women should either function within roles assigned by men or women should express their freedom to fully be who they are.

Should physical sex be surgically altered? What are appropriate visible expressions of social identity as a male or female? Psychologists and moralists debate the wisdom of altering someone's physical sex through surgery. Cultural norms either narrowly or broadly suggest appropriate visible expressions of social identity, of a man's or woman's sexually specific appearance. People of faith argue passionately over religious design. Is there such a thing as religious design, a design that either limits what women should do or establishes the full equality of women and men? Are women restricted in any way men are not? Or are women and men equally free to live as they choose in both church and society, of course within mutually agreed-upon and nondiscriminatively applied moral boundaries?

While these questions clamor for attention, another one, perhaps more important, waits in the wings to be addressed: What does it mean to relate as feminine women and masculine men for the glory of God?

Did God create us male and female to relate in unique ways that together reveal the glory of how God relates, within His own community and with us? That is the question raised by the idea of *relational gender*. It was a question I wanted to ask, and this book is my effort to engage with that question. Let's begin at the beginning. Genesis 1:26–27 is our starting point.

2

WORDS HAVE MEANING

Then God said, "Let us make human beings in our image, to be like us". . . .
So God created human beings in his own image. In the image of God he
created them; male and female he created them.

Genesis 1:26–27 NLT

Words that seem difficult to understand at first glance are sometimes worth
a second look, maybe even a third. For example, consider these words
written by theologian Reinhold Niebuhr, who tells us the "eternal is revealed in the temporal but not exhausted by it."[1] Do you find those words
confusing? I do. But think with me. Consider: If the *eternal* is relational
because God is a timeless community of three persons in heaven, and if the
temporal consists centrally of male and female persons relating on earth
in community, then could it be that men and women relating together in
this world are intended to provide a glimpse of the relational life of the
Trinity? Are we designed as gendered beings to reveal something about
how the eternal God relates by the unique ways we relate?

1. Reinhold Niebuhr, *Beyond Tragedy: Essays on the Christian Interpretation of History*,
quoted in Brian D. Ingraffe, *Postmodern Theory and Biblical Theology* (Cambridge: Cambridge
University Press, 1995) 86.

Well-Disguised Selfishness

Self-centeredness is a many-headed Medusa. Before God's Spirit pours Christ's life into us, selfishness is the primary energy in the human soul. Scratch beneath the surface of most of the words we say and an obsessive concern with our well-being will show itself, a concern that is willingly committed to using others, including God, for self-centered purposes. The old cliché still speaks truth: it's all about us.

I've asked dozens of women when they feel most feminine, most glad to be alive as a woman, most womanly. Several were offended when I used the word *femininity*. One expressed herself strongly and with angry passion. "Your question is demeaning. Asking me when I feel feminine implies I'm supposed to be attractive to a man, more a 'girly object' than a respected person. Listen! I'm as much a person as any man. What I do, how I think, and who I am matters more than how I look."

More typical responses came after a confused expression and a thoughtful pause: "I'm not sure I've ever really asked myself that question." When I would press a bit, several women smiled and said, "Well, I do feel good about myself as a woman when I know I look nice." Others thought the experience of pregnancy and giving birth was an embodiment of their unique identity as women. A few said they felt most feminine during the act of sex. Still others expressed their desire to be wanted, valued, and respected, by both men and women, for their minds and their competence, for what they could offer to others and to society.

Not one woman told me, "I feel most fully alive as a feminine woman when I relate to others in a way that reveals something wonderful about God, something wonderful about how He relates that I was specially designed as a woman to make known."

I've asked dozens of men, mostly Christians, when they feel most masculine, most alive as men. The majority responded with a look of amused indifference. Some grinned and said, "What do you think I am? A wimp?" or "The evidence is pretty clear. I'm not a woman. And I'm not gay." More serious responses to the question had to do with competence, achievement, status, athletic ability, a winning and fun personality in business meetings or locker rooms, and recognition, mostly from male peers.

Not one man (including me, at least before I began writing this book) came even close to saying, "I feel most alive as a masculine man when I relate to others in a way that reveals something unbelievably good about God, something awesome about how He relates that I was specially designed as a man to make known."

What makes a woman feminine? What makes a man masculine? Like few others, those two questions reveal a well-disguised self-centeredness that keeps the God who created everything for His glory in a comfortably vague religious background and spotlights whatever we possess or control that lets us feel good about ourselves. No value feels greater than our experienced well-being.

That same energy fuels much of the gender debate roaring through our culture. Almost always, political correctness mandates that gender identity be wrapped up in freedom, not a God-empowered liberty to reveal Him but a self-interested personal entitlement to make much of ourselves: "Don't define women by the sexy models on magazine covers and don't define men by the width of a linebacker's shoulders. Women are feminine and men are masculine, if anyone really cares about such matters, when they exercise their freedom to live, look, and relate any way they want to, to make whatever choices enhance their sense of personal worth." Full personhood, not full genderedness, is the issue.

Religious correctness, in Christian circles, comes mostly in two versions. The traditional version teaches that godly women express their God-designed womanhood by submitting to their husbands at home and to the leadership of men in church. And they do so in obedience to God, with sincere desire to honor Him. Women without husbands are free to move through society as they wish but must submit to male authority in ministry. Femininity, if the word is used at all, is revealed in a woman conforming to her God-appointed role. Masculinity, again a rarely used word, has more to do with the strong, loving exercise of male leadership in the family and in church, and to some degree in professional and business circles.

Egalitarianism, the second version of religious correctness in the Christian world, understands the submission and silence passages in the Bible (Eph. 5:22–24 and 1 Tim. 2:9–12) as instructions that speak into a cultural situation that no longer exists today. Appealing to Scripture, evangelical egalitarians believe they are honoring God and His gospel by encouraging women and men (particularly women) to enjoy their Christ-won freedom to live as free and equal persons. Mature womanhood centers in freedom and equality, not submission and silence. Mature manhood reveals itself in a man's refusal to subject women to his supposed authority and in his freedom to pursue his calling as he lives in equality with women in home, church, and society.

None of the "correct" views on gender seem to vigorously wrestle with how the Bible might define a *feminine* woman or a *masculine* man. As I hope to show, biblical words combine with stories and instructions in the Bible to indicate that femininity and masculinity consist of unique and deeply embedded *ways of relating*. This idea that feminine women and masculine men are wired to relate to others in a way that reveals something unique about God's relational character is not easily digested, in part perhaps because living the idea requires an assault on our self-centeredness. The primary passion to reveal God to others at any cost to ourselves requires that our self-obsession give way to God-obsession.

If the Bible does support that idea, then it must be explored. Before we wonder whether we are feminine women or masculine men, before we interpret the submission and silence passages, and before we decide whether we are in the traditional or the egalitarian camp, we should study God's choice of words when He refers to His creation of us as male and female persons. Perhaps that study will provide further leads to understand how He has designed women and men to relate, and for what purpose. Words do have meaning, especially biblical words.

A Relational Understanding of Gender: First Hints

Look again at two familiar verses. Notice the words I've italicized.

> Then God said, "*Let us* make *human beings* in our image, *to be like us. They* will reign over the fish in the sea, the birds in the sky, the livestock, all the wild animals on the earth, and the small animals that scurry along the ground."

> So God created human beings in his own image.
> In the image of God he created them;
> *male and female* he created them. (Gen. 1:26–27 NLT)

It should not be missed that the biblical story assumes—it does not bother to prove—God's existence. What is self-evident to a humble mind needs no defense. Right away, we're told that the God who has always existed created everything that is now in existence. Beginning in verse 3 and continuing through verse 25, the first chapter of the Genesis narrative simply says that seven times God spoke a word and everything from light to space to oceans to plants, fish, birds, and animals miraculously appeared. In these verses, there are no direct references to who God is, only to what He can do.

But the formula changes when He creates human beings. Now God is recorded as saying, for the first time, "Let us," apparently referring to a conversation between at least two, perhaps three, divine persons that led to a joint decision. It's significant to observe that the first hint of God as *a community of persons* occurs when He creates people. And the God who chooses at this point, no sooner, to reveal Himself as a relational divine being creates human beings *to be like Him*. How? In His relationality? It would seem so. The relational divine being creates relational human beings. That's how the story of God—and of humans—begins.

The implications go to the very root of who we are and how we are designed to live. God eternally exists in relationship. He is a relational being, and Scripture goes on to reveal that deity consists of three distinct persons living in community. (It might be noticed in passing that the Trinity is the only small group that has ever gotten along really well and for a really long time.)

Because this relational God created us to be like Him, from the moment each of us came into existence we were created as relational beings, called and designed to live in God-like community as distinct male and female persons.

Notice, too, the word *they* in verse 26: "they will reign . . ." Over what? Over "the fish in the sea, the birds in the sky, the livestock, all the wild animals on the earth, and the small animals that scurry along the ground." Apparently, men and women together are granted equal authority to rule over all subhuman life. But no mention is made of one gender ruling over the other. At least at this point, the issue of authority doesn't seem to enter into God's plan for how His image-bearers are to get along with each other.

And then in verse 27, the inspired writer repeats himself, a means of emphasizing something. "So God created human beings in his own image. In the image of God he created them." The point is clear: we were created to be like God! Not to be God, but in some crucial way to resemble God.

The writer then immediately tells us that God made us male and female. To be like the beyond-gender God in our gender? Again, it seems so. And because it is only when God made male and female human beings that He introduced Himself as persons-in-community ("Let *us*"), we are encouraged to assume that *it is as male and female persons that we are like God in His relational nature.*

We now have reason to think that whatever it means to be masculine or feminine, relating as the Trinity does is at least part of the picture—and perhaps the picture itself.

To briefly summarize:

- God first revealed Himself to be a community of persons-in-relationship, not when He created the heavens and the earth; the stars, suns, and planets; the plants, fish, birds, and animals, but only when He created male and female persons.
- At creation, He gave the persons He made equal authority over all subhuman life, but no ruling authority over each other.
- As a God revealed as relational, He made male and female persons to be like Him, opening the possibility that men and women are to relate with each other in a way that resembles how the persons of the Trinity relate.

With these beginning thoughts in mind, we can now more carefully explore God's purpose in making us male and female. In the process, we'll discover what it means to be a feminine woman or a masculine man and move ahead to a careful look at the key words in these two verses in Genesis, in their original language.

3

In the Beginning

Gender in the Garden of Eden

Deep longings lie dormant in the unawakened soul. Souls stay asleep in order to avoid feeling pain and facing failure. But an alive and sustaining sense of purpose that survives the inevitable disappointments and tragedies of life is available to every person who wakes up to discover his or her gendered center.

I wonder if God will welcome my wife into heaven by warmly saying, "Well done! You lived your life as a beautiful woman, feminine to the core." I think He will.

To some women, I fear He will say, "Like everyone whom I gladly receive to live with Me forever, you are here because My Son died to give you the gift of eternal life. But although you lived your life as a friendly, attractive, charming, moral, generous, hardworking, and competent woman, very few in your circle of family and friends were drawn to Me by the way you related to them. The core beauty of your soul remained hidden. You did not live as a deeply feminine woman." On that day, no woman will say, "What are You talking about?" They will know. Then.

Mother Teresa

A framed pencil sketch of Mother Teresa hangs in our hallway. I walk by it every day. More often than not, I pause and look. And when I do, it never fails:

every time I feel strangely captured by an awareness of indescribable beauty, a beauty that opens the eyes of my soul to see and appreciate what my natural sight can neither see nor appreciate. I look at Mother Teresa and I want God.

Why? Was the worn-out, wrinkled saint of Calcutta beautiful with the beauty of God? Was she feminine? Listen to Peter as he talks to wives. His words speak to all women, married or single, and they describe Mother Teresa.

> Don't be concerned about the outward beauty of fancy hairstyles, expensive jewelry, or beautiful clothes. You should clothe yourselves instead with the beauty that comes from within, the unfading beauty of a gentle and quiet spirit, which is so precious to God. This is how the holy women of old made themselves beautiful. (1 Pet. 3:3–5 NLT)

Beauty that comes from within. Unfading beauty. The beauty of a gentle and quiet spirit. Holy women making themselves beautiful.

It is, I think, safe to assume that Mother Teresa now belongs to the group of holy women that Peter mentioned. The question then is: How did she make herself beautiful? Certainly not with the latest hairstyles, diamond earrings, or expensive gowns. A man looks at a "sex goddess" and lusts. A man looks at a feminine woman and worships. If he has eyes that can see true beauty, sexual attraction to a feminine woman, no matter how strong, takes a backseat to worshiping God and enjoying the feminine woman's way of relating with others.

Mother Teresa sacrificially and with single-mindedness served others. Her life purpose was to bring the lost to Jesus and to bring Jesus to the lost. But a man can just as well live for that same purpose. Can a woman serve others in a different way than a man, with a different relational energy, whether she's preaching from behind a pulpit or hugging children in an orphanage? Was there something *womanly* about the way Mother Teresa reached out to India's poorest?

I was once privileged to hear Mother Teresa speak at a Washington, DC, prayer breakfast. As I sat there with three thousand others who were listening to her frail but somehow still strong voice, I watched as she opened her arms and said, "Don't kill more unborn babies. Let them live, then bring them to me." As she spoke, I could see Jesus with outstretched arms speaking words of invitation, "Come to me, all of you who are weary and carry heavy burdens, and I will give you rest" (Matt. 11:28 NLT).

The beauty of femininity spread the aroma of God throughout that auditorium, a beauty in Mother Teresa's words that corresponded to something beautiful in God, which Jesus perfectly revealed.

Three Words to Think About

Invitational power is alive in the soul of every woman who knows Jesus. She has a power to reveal the relational nature of God that no man can reveal as clearly. Call it feminine power. It's not sexual appeal. It's not a socially winsome personality, or physical beauty, or ambition-driven competence. It's the beauty of relational femininity. The book of Genesis will help us understand this concept.

> Then God said, "Let us make man [*adam*] in our image, after our likeness." (Gen. 1:26)

> With the LORD's help, I have produced a man [*ish*]. (4:1 NLT)

> She will be called "woman" [*ishah*], because she was taken from "man." (2:23 NLT)

Adam

The first word to notice is *adam*. It's more than the first man's name. In Hebrew, *adam* simply refers to a human being, whether male or female; a human person, not a divine person or an animal creature but a man or woman made in the image of God. Then God said, "Let us make Adam, in our image, to be like us" (see 1:26).

Let *us*, the three persons in the divine community, make human beings *to be like us,* as relational beings.

The Scriptures say God is love. God is a relational being whose love was poured out within His own community of the Trinity before anything or anyone else existed. His essential glory, His *relational* glory, is to love, to give, to enhance the joy and well-being of another at any cost to Himself. To reveal His glory, God created human beings who, like Him, are capable of giving and receiving love. He created us to love us, and to empower us to reveal His love by the way we relate to others. His plan was that we would live together as persons-in-community the way the Trinity lives together as persons-in-community.

Ish

The second word we need to notice is the Hebrew word *ish*. When Eve gave birth—a new and delightfully surprising experience that uniquely belonged to her as a woman—she said, "With the Lord's help, I have produced [*ish*], a man" (4:1 NLT). But she was holding a baby. Why did she call the infant a man? Her baby was a human being whose anatomy matched her husband's, not hers. She recognized that her firstborn was a male human, a baby boy that would grow up to be a man. She could as easily have said, "I have produced a man-in-the-making, a male person."

When she declared that her child was *ish*, she was speaking of his biological sex, not his relational masculinity. The issue of *gender* was yet to be revealed.

Ishah

The third word to notice is *ishah*. When Adam woke up from his nap, he saw a creature unlike all the animals he had named before he fell asleep, a fellow *adam*, a human being like him, but not *ish*, not a male. "This at last is bone of my bones and flesh of my flesh; she shall be called Woman [*ishah*] because she was taken out of Man [*ish*]" (2:23).

I imagine his excitement was twofold. One, he sensed right away that there was now someone he could relationally enjoy in a way he was not able to with the dogs and monkeys and bears he had just named.

But his excitement had a second source, certainly sexual but also personal and relational. There was something enticing about this fellow *adam*. This person was like him, but different and appealing. With unspoiled wisdom, Adam recognized something that inspired him to say, "She will be called *ishah* because she was taken from *ish*."

Again, *sex* is in view, not *gender*. Not yet. Femaleness was clear. Femininity remained to be revealed and enjoyed.

Two More Words

If there were no further words to discuss, if femininity and masculinity were not somehow yet to be revealed as the relational expressions of sex, then gender would be identified by the necessary, universal, physical expressions of a person's biologic sex: of *adam* as either *ish* or *ishah*. A person's gender would then amount to nothing more than voice pitch, hairstyle, body shape, and clothing. Gender would be reduced mostly to sexuality, to physical characteristics in one that aroused physical excitement in another, or at least to social compatibility.

Soul communion would be lost. The quality of a relationship would be measured by the level of felt satisfaction one person experienced in the presence of another. The satisfaction would be derived from either common interests or sexual arousal, or both. The door would then swing open to same-sex or opposite-sex meetings of any kind, sexual or social. Even good friends would fall short of God's relational glory. Naked bodies would try to provide the passion that was no longer available in entwined souls. Golfing buddies and church friends would then survive on less satisfaction than God intended and only vaguely realize what they were missing.

The Bible does, however, offer more words that open up a relational understanding of gender, an understanding of relational femininity and masculinity, and point the way toward a meeting of souls that satisfies far more deeply than a meeting of bodies or a meeting of mutual interests.

Listen to Genesis 1:26–27 once again, with my clarifying comments:

> "Let us, a community of relational persons, make human beings (*adam*) in our image, not as physical beings but as relational beings, to be like us in the way we relate."
>
> So God created human persons (*adam*) in his own relational image, with the God-like capacity to enjoy the kind of relational pleasure in human community that God enjoys in His divine community. In the image of a profoundly happy relational God he created them, male (*zakar*) and female (*neqebah*) he created them.

With these two Hebrew words, *zakar* and *neqebah*, the idea of gender is introduced as the relational expression of a person's sex. We'll look first at *neqebah*, a word that takes us further than *ishah*, into what makes a woman feminine. Mother Teresa was a human person (*adam*) and a female (*ishah*), but she was also feminine (*neqebah*). What does that mean?

4

WHAT MAKES A WOMAN FEMININE?

And yet in our world everybody thinks of changing the world but nobody thinks of changing himself.

Leo Tolstoy[1]

Everybody can be great because everybody can serve.

Dr. Martin Luther King Jr.[2]

In this world we cannot all do great things; we can only do small things with great love.

Mother Teresa[3]

Who is more important, the one who sits at the table or the one who serves? The one who sits at the table, of course. But not here! For I am among you as one who serves.

Jesus Christ (Luke 22:27 NLT)

1. Leo Tolstoy, *Pamphlets* (Ann Arbor: University of Michigan, 1900), 29.
2. Dr. Martin Luther King Jr., Speech Delivered at Ebenezer Baptist Church, Atlanta, Georgia, February 4, 1968.
3. Mother Teresa and Brian Kolodiejchuk, *Mother Teresa: Come Be My Light* (New York: Doubleday Religion, 2007).

What makes a woman feminine? The ideas about gender that I will develop are foreign to the way much of our Christian culture thinks and are severely inconsistent with secular culture, and might therefore be resisted or quickly dismissed.

Ponder this beginning thought: a woman is feminine when she relates in a way that invites others to see something about God that is irresistibly attractive, something about the relational nature of God that she was created to enjoy and reveal. I believe this is an accurate and biblical view, contrary to what society has presented. And to begin, let me offer a few words of biblical context to define what I mean when I use the term "relational femininity."

A Relational God

Jesus told us to love each other the way He loves us, to put His way of relating on display by the way we relate (see John 13:34–35). His plan is clear. He intends to parade His compelling love for the world to see, not only by the social activism of His followers but also, and more so, by how closely the way His followers relate to each other corresponds to the way Jesus relates.

This is radical stuff. Think about the last time someone hurt your feelings. What happened in you? How did you respond? Paul wants us to display the same attitude that Jesus had, an attitude that was willing to suffer terrible treatment without retaliation, for one purpose: *to reveal the relational glory of God* (see Phil. 2:5–11).

Can you and I, ordinary men and women, living with all the slights and snubs and stings that come in even the best of relationships, actually internalize that attitude and live it every day as we relate with each other? Jesus seemed to think so.

> "I have given them [His followers, you and me] the glory you gave me [the special favor of God that came with Christ's incarnation, the opportunity to suffer betrayal and abandonment in order to reveal God's love in human relating, in any circumstance, in every relationship], so they [you and I] may be one as we are one." (John 17:22 NLT)

Think about that last phrase, "*so they may be one as we are one*." Jesus prayed that human beings (*adam*), men and women (*ish* and *ishah*), would reproduce divine community in human community, never perfectly but more and more easily recognizable as divine, Trinitarian, and God-like. He wants us to meet on the bridge built by His cross, the bridge on which men and women can connect by relating to each other in a way that reveals how God relates. We are to make known the God that every human being was created to enjoy, the God that wants us to join His party and start dancing with each other.

Now here's the point I'm moving toward. Human community is made up of men and women relating. We are sexual beings, *ish* and *ishah*, physical beings who can talk together, work together, play together, enjoy physical intimacy together, live together, and serve in our churches and communities together. But we can do more.

We *are* more. We are relationally gendered, spiritual beings designed by God to meet on the bridge by revealing, as feminine women and masculine men, something wonderfully unique about God's relational nature. We reveal something that lets us see why the three persons of the Trinity connect so well, why they are eternally happy with a joy that they long to share with us.

Earlier, we looked at three Hebrew words: *adam* (human persons), *ish* (male persons), and *ishah* (female persons). Together, these three words state the obvious: people are human persons who come in two sexes, male and female. And because we bear a relational God's image, we are built to connect and relate with each other, not just physically but personally.

But how? How are we to connect, to successfully relate together? Let's turn to two more Hebrew words: *neqebah* and *zakar*, words that occur in the original language of Genesis: "So God created human beings in his own image. In the image of God he created them; male (*zakar*) and female (*neqebah*) he created them" (1:27 NLT).

We already know what's obvious: we are men or women. But these two words will now lead us into less obvious and more controversial territory, into what it means to be like God as relationally gendered.

Neqebah: Toward an Understanding of Femininity

A feminine woman is—what? Sensual? Nurturing? Tender? Svelte? When God first introduces us to women, He refers to them as *neqebah*. The word means "punctured; bored through."

Huh? A feminine woman is a woman who has been punctured? At best, that's confusing. At worst, it's offensive. Where is this word taking us?

Less literally, *neqebah* refers to something that has been opened and can now be entered. Is God wanting us to think of the way He designed a woman's body? In sex, the most physically intimate act, the woman presents her body, opened by God, capable of being entered by a man's body. The meeting is productive and pleasurable, and blessed by God if the man and woman are in covenant relationship, married, committed to each other for life, and committed to the other's pleasure more than their own.

A thought comes to mind: perhaps the physical shape of a woman's body is a kind of parable, or picture, of the spiritual shape of a woman's soul. Could femininity have something to do with a woman who is *relationally* opened to receive? Our likeness to God is not physical. God is a spiritual being, three persons who relate together not physically but personally. We reflect Him most clearly as we relate together as persons.

Neqebah *suggests that femininity is relational.*

A feminine woman is a woman who relates in a particular way; she is opened to receive others who come to her. And, pushing the image further, she warmly and pleasurably surrounds those whom she receives. She invites movement toward her and embraces the movement she receives.

Neqebah *suggests women are designed to invite, to neither demand nor control.*

When Eve sinned in the garden, God's judgment came in two parts: *physical pain*, pain in pregnancy and in childbirth, both the result of physical intimacy; and *relational pain*, conflict on the bridge, a man and woman each vying for control. "Eve," God said, "you will now desire to control your husband. But he won't like it. He'll prove you can't control him by backing away from you. Or he might try to dominate you into submission" (see Gen. 3:16).

Several translations of Genesis 3:16 put it this way: "your desire will be for your husband." However, the word so often translated *desire* in Genesis 3:16, *teshuqah*, occurs again in Genesis 4:7, where God is speaking to Cain, warning him that his unwarranted and selfish resentment of his brother could lead to violence. "Sin is crouching at the door, *eager to control* you" (NLT, emphasis added). The word translated *desire* in God's judgment on Eve is the same word in God's warning to Cain, translated *eager to control*. The New Living Translation of Genesis 3:16 has it right: "you will desire to control your husband."

God was judging Eve as a woman, both as a physical woman and as a relational woman. A relationally feminine woman is open to receive. She doesn't demand, she invites like Jesus, who invited weary people to come to Him. But Eve, now an unfeminine woman, is closed. She is no longer open to receive but now is eager to control.

Why? God's judgment was not arbitrary. It was a natural consequence of her retreating from God in disobedience. Refusing to trustingly rest in God's love, neither depending on nor enjoying His goodness, Eve was now on her own, vulnerable in a dangerous relational world. She needed from Adam what she could not guarantee, what she could no longer enjoy from God. With God out of the picture, Adam would now have to do. But he might hurt her. He had already blamed her for his failure. Of course she had to protect herself by gaining the upper hand. That's entirely reasonable—to a woman who doesn't know God.

Eve was no longer open to receive. She was now eager to control, defensively and insistently. Her relational fragrance was no longer invitational. It was now spoiled by demand, a spirit of entitlement: "You should come through for me. You *must* come through for me. I'll see to it you do, and leave you if you don't." Eve, and the daughters of Eve, became unfeminine women. Only God could restore their femininity. Only the implanted life of Jesus could empower them to relate like Jesus, to invite, to neither demand nor control, and to ultimately and finally depend on and enjoy God, not people and especially not men.

Neqebah *suggests a feminine woman discerns and is open to receive only what reflects God's character and advances His purposes.*

This thought comes out of an Old Testament story told in 2 Kings 12. Joash, King of Judah, realized it was important to repair the Lord's temple. His people were no longer worshiping in the place God wanted them to worship. Instead, they were offering their sacrifices at pagan shrines. The temple was not in good shape. But repairs required funds. So Joash commissioned the priests to collect the money people gave to the Lord and use it to pay for the badly needed repairs.

After a delay, a priest named Jehoiada finally got around to doing what the king wanted done: collecting money. He "bored a hole in the lid of a large chest and set it on the right-hand side of the altar at the entrance of the Temple of the Lord. The priests guarding the entrance put all of the people's contributions into the chest," through the opening made in its lid (v. 9 NLT). With the money put into the opened chest, the temple was restored.

Jehoiada "bored a hole" in the lid of the chest. That phrase translates a word closely related to *neqebah*. The chest was opened to receive. But notice that it was opened to receive only what people who were obeying God put into the opening. And nothing entered through the opened chest that was not used to advance God's purposes. The temple was restored and that pleased God.

The story suggests an important lesson: when God opens something, He opens it as part of a plan to receive only what brings glory to Himself by revealing His character and advancing His purposes. Through Jehoiada's obedience, God opened the chest to arrange for the restoration of true worship. When He opens a woman, He opens her to receive only what reveals His character and advances His purposes.

> Neqebah *suggests relational femininity is a two-way street. It includes an openness to receive and a willingness to give.*

The Gospel writer Mark tells the story of a debate between some Pharisees and Jesus. The winner, of course, was Jesus. The Pharisees had challenged the Lord to explain and defend His views on divorce. Moses, God's appointed law-giver, had given permission for a man to "give his wife a written notice of divorce and send her away" (see Mark 10:2–9 NLT). Did Jesus agree? Would He take issue with Moses?

In our Lord's response, He reminded His challengers that "God made them male and female from the beginning" (Mark 10:6 NLT) and pressed the point that connection, not distance, was God's plan. *Thēlus*, the Greek word used for "female" in this passage, refers to the female breast, more specifically the nipple on the breast. Figuratively, *thēlus* implies something with the capacity to nourish, *to release into another what can sustain another's life.*

Physical femininity is centered in the capacity to receive and give, a body opened to be entered and to bring life through procreation, and breasts released to pour out nourishment that sustains life.

Relational femininity is a way of relating that both invites life-giving connection from another and nourishes life-giving relating in another. But this is only a preliminary understanding of relational femininity, a beginning definition. Much more can—and will—be said.

To appreciate how liberating God's calling to women really is, we need to think through what Peter had in mind when he instructed wives to submit to their husbands. His words were addressed specifically to married women but they speak to all women, with a surprising understanding of what it means for a woman to submit.

We hear the word *submit* and think stifling restriction. When God says the word *submit*, it opens an opportunity to reveal something wonderful about the way He relates.

5

SUBMISSION

A Dirty Word?

Then God said, "Let us make man in our image (*tselem*), after our likeness (*demut*)."

Genesis 1:26

Every human being bears the image and likeness of God. That means we were created both to *represent* God by reflecting His Trinitarian existence in this world as bearers of His *tselem*, his image, and to *resemble* God as bearers of His *demut*, His relational likeness, by relating in our community the way God relates in His community.

Women and men are specially designed by God to bring Him glory by both reflecting back to God and revealing to each other something unique about the way our three-person God relates within His divine family and with His human family.

From all eternity, each person of the Trinity *gives* to the other two and *receives* from the other two, always *moving* toward the others to give and always remaining *open* to receive.

And that is how God relates to us, always moving toward us to give us everything we need and always open to receive from us everything it brings us joy to give.

Mutual Submission

Wives, submit. There's no way around it. God tells women to submit to their husbands. But it's also true that God instructs men to submit to their wives. His plan seems to be that husbands and wives live in a relationship of *mutual* submission.

But how each submits to the other is different. Feminine women submit one way. Masculine men submit another way. What's the difference?

The traditional answer to that question goes something like this: husbands submit to the needs of their "weaker" wives (the word *weaker* is in 1 Pet. 3:7) by firmly, strongly, and kindly leading them in good directions. For men, submission centers in loving *authority*. Wives, on the other hand, submit to their husbands by warmly following their husband's leadership. For women, submission means loving *obedience*.

Take it a step further: there are to be no exceptions to a woman's obedience, as Paul made clear. "Now as the church submits to Christ, so also wives should submit *in everything* to their husbands" (Eph. 5:24, emphasis mine). Those words are in the text. There's no getting around it. But what do those words mean?

The meaning I was taught in younger days made me glad to join Jewish men in thanking God every day that I was not born a woman. It seemed to me that Paul (Peter as well) was confronting women with a difficult choice. Either wives were to hunker down under God's orders and do whatever their godly or ungodly husbands told them to do, or they must disobey God and take matters into their own competent hands, standing up for themselves as equal partners in all relationships.

I suppose there is a third option, one casually chosen by increasing numbers of Christian women: just don't bother with the issue. Let seminary professors and scholarly pastors figure out what submission means. Stick with practical ideas about how to make a marriage work without worrying about all that sophisticated Bible teaching. The day-to-day challenges of getting along are hard enough without a wife having to think about whether she is being submissive or not. At worst, submission is an obnoxious idea. At best, it's an antique better suited to a century ago. It just isn't all that relevant to keeping a marriage alive. Is that right?

Is *submission* really an offensively dirty word that makes unreasonable and demeaning demands on women?

That can't be. God never speaks a word that dishonors His creation. His commands may sound offensive to our proud self-centeredness, but never to our humble self-surrender. Every word that comes from the mouth of God is a word by which we can live fully alive as women and men. His words are good and pure, fair and beautiful, always life-giving and never life-smothering.

But *submission*? Is it fair and just? Is a good and beautiful life lived when a woman submits to her husband? Yes, of course . . . if we understand submission rightly. Perhaps we need to more closely examine what God had in mind when He told women to submit to their husbands. And what does submission have to do with a woman becoming fully alive in her femininity for the glory of God?

Correcting the Misunderstanding

I stand first in line as a man who badly needed to rethink what God meant when He told my wife to submit to me.

Nearly fifty years ago, as I listened to a beautiful, talented, and competent woman vow to obey me, I felt a rush of superiority. My vows in front of the preacher on our wedding day didn't include the "o" word. I pledged to cherish my wife, not obey her.

As I listened to the promises we made to each other, an image popped into my mind. I saw myself as a friendly but firm sergeant looking at a female private who, for her own good, was required to do what I said. Of course I also could hear myself vowing to love Rachael the way Christ loved His bride, the church. I felt no inconsistency between my roles as sergeant and lover.

Why? I was the man, called to love by leading. She was the woman, called to love by submitting. I directed. She followed. That was the plan, and I liked it. It made me feel strong, masculine, alive in my manhood with my broad shoulders back and my proud head held high.

I felt good, but I also felt pressure. Like a surgeon directing a nurse as they perform open-heart surgery, I had to get it right. Like the nurse, my wife's job was to follow my lead, no questions asked and advice given only on request. And like the surgeon, my responsibility was to make no mistakes. One slip on my part could mean our patient's death.

Could I always get it right? I felt scared, inadequate for the job, more weak than confidently strong. Did I have what it would take to lead my wife through conflict, through parenting fears, through decisions about money and career, through the inevitable struggles on the narrow road to life? I wasn't sure.

Even now as I write these words nearly a half century later, I wonder if those doubts were the first stirrings of a desire for a marriage partner, not a subordinate. I recently asked Rachael how she was feeling as my views on submission were changing. Her response required less than a second of thought. "Relief," she said.

It's time for us to clean up a word that, thanks to our backgrounds and fallen natures, too often sounds like a dirty word in our ears. Two passages in particular are helping me to see the word *submission* shine with its intended beauty, for both women and men. In our culture, the really hard question is this: Should a wife submit to her husband in everything? My answer is: of course. That's what Scripture says. But my question is: What does Scripture mean?

The first of the two passages I want us to look at is half of a verse in Genesis. Adam, before God created Eve, was told to name all the animals. I wonder if Adam finished his task feeling incredibly lonely. *These are the only living creatures I can hang out with? Something is missing.* I imagine God chuckling in anticipation as He directed the following words to be written: "for Adam there was not found a helper fit for him" (Gen. 2:20). Some translations read that no helper "suitable" for Adam was found among the animals. If God was chuckling, it was a laugh of joy. He knew the surprise that awaited Adam.

Now I suppose a chauvinist, a man who feels superior to women, or worse, a misogynist, a man who looks down on women with hateful scorn, might glibly conclude that this passage proves that God agrees with his terrible views on women. The text is clear: women are made by God to be suitable helpers for men. Men like sex. Our wives should make themselves available for our pleasure when and how we want it. Men like food. Our wives should learn how to cook meals that we enjoy.

It's a woman's place to cooperate with wherever our careers take us, to follow our lead in how to parent our kids, to spend money as we want it spent. Good men, of course, should be reasonable and sensitive, occasionally even tender. But the bottom line is clear: a wife exists to be a suitable helper for her husband. That's what the text says.

But is that what the text means? Not even close.

Ezer

The word translated "helper" is *ezer*. That's a Hebrew word used throughout the Old Testament to refer to God! It's in Exodus 18:4; Deuteronomy 33:7, 26, 29; Psalm 33:20; 115:9–11; 124:8; and 140:5. The Exodus passage tells us that Moses named his second son Eliezer, a name that means "God is my helper." And we know why Moses chose that name. It's in Exodus 18: "for he said, 'The God of my father was my help, and delivered me from the sword of Pharaoh'"(v. 4). Moses remembered God's powerful intervention in his life and said, "God was my *ezer*."

Eve was Adam's *ezer*.

Notice this: *the word* ezer *is never used to refer to a subordinate serving a superior, certainly not when it is used to refer to God as our helper.* In the Greek translation of the Old Testament, *ezer* is translated as *boēthos*. That word literally means "help provided by someone strong."

Does this imply wives are as strong as their husbands, maybe stronger? But didn't Peter tell men to show "honor to the woman as the *weaker* vessel" (1 Pet. 3:7, emphasis mine)? It's true that most women are physically weaker than most men and are therefore more vulnerable to physical and sexual abuse. And women tend to more easily acknowledge when they feel hurt and might therefore appear in some instances to be emotionally weaker than men. Are those observations what Peter had in mind?

Remember, it's also true that women display incredible strength that no man understands in moving through the excruciating pain of childbirth and in climbing out of bed at two in the morning to care for a screaming infant while her husband snores away. Of course women are strong in many ways, in some ways stronger than men.

But I wonder if *ezer* and *boēthos* tell us something more about women. As I have already suggested, women are designed to reveal something about God more clearly (can we say more strongly?) than men. Could this be a strong ability to imitate God's invitational nature, even to critical and rejecting men, and could that ability have something to do with a woman being an *ezer*, a *boēthos*, a strong helper?

That may be too speculative. But what is clear is that there is no hint of subordination born of weakness in the words *ezer* or *boēthos*. Look now at another word in our text.

Kenegdo

Eve was created to be a helper (*ezer*) suitable for Adam. *Kenegdo* is the Hebrew word translated "fit" or "suitable." It refers to someone who corresponds to another, someone who is uniquely designed to come alongside another as a companion—neither behind as a follower nor beneath as an inferior.

Remember the Bridge of Connection? Adam stands on one end of the bridge, alone with a zoo full of animals. If no fellow human stands on the other end of the bridge, Adam has no suitable helper to give to, to love, to be helped by, or to enjoy. He would then be destined to live for himself and to arrange his life on earth around his needs because no one else exists with human needs. He would always be aware of relational needs in himself that could never begin to be satisfied in a world with beautiful flowers and interesting animals but with no other human person capable of receiving what he can give and giving what he longs to receive.

But Adam awoke from a nap and looked across the bridge to see a fellow human, a suitable helper, an *ishah* that corresponded to him, an *ish*—a strong woman who could invite Adam to move toward her as a strong man, who could reveal the openness of an invitational God. I imagine that scene in paradise when Adam met Eve, and I want to shout, "Let the dance begin!" My response mirrors God's. When God saw a man and a woman in the middle of His beautiful creation, He sang the Bible's first song: "Then God looked over all he had made, and he saw that it was very good," not just good, but *very* good (Gen. 1:31 NLT). His kingdom had come to earth.

The first passage in Genesis points us toward a new way of understanding a woman's submission, a new way that cleans the dirt off the word and reveals its beauty. The phrase "suitable helper" tells us that no woman by virtue of her gender is inferior to man.

Skipping ahead to new covenant teaching, we can say with confidence that every Christ-following woman is equipped by Christ's Spirit to advance the purposes of Christ's Father. How? By relating with the courage and strength of a suitable helper, corresponding to how God helped Moses escape the sword of Pharaoh to lead his people to the Promised Land.

But the question remains: Exactly what does it mean for a woman to submit to her husband in everything? Can our study of *ezer* and *kenegdo* lead us into a cleaned up and liberating understanding of submission?

To answer those questions, we must now look at a second passage, this one longer and full of wisdom. I'll need another chapter to unpack what I hear Peter telling us about a wife's submission to her husband, and to move closer to knowing what it means for a woman, single or married, to be fully alive in her femininity for the glory of God. It gets a bit tricky, but stay with me. Where we're leading is good. It's *very* good.

6

WHAT SUBMISSION REALLY MEANS

The challenge of the Christian life is to act toward others in ways that are similar to the way that God has acted toward us.

Charles Ringma[1]

The Worth and Excellency of a soul is to be measured by the object of its love.

Henry Scougal[2]

"My husband just admitted to me that he's addicted to pornography. I have no idea what it would mean to submit to him. And I feel anything but feminine. I feel so unwanted, in every way. I can't imagine ever respecting him again."

"My husband's ideas about parenting are really over the top. He says he believes in strict discipline, but he comes down so hard on our kids that he's driving them away from him. And he's always on my case for being too lenient. There's no way I can go along with a kind of discipline that makes my kids terrified to be around their father. Am I really expected to submit to him?"

1. Charles Ringma, *Seize the Day with Dietrich Bonhoeffer* (Colorado Springs, CO: Pinon Press, 2000), January 3.

2. Henry Scougal, *The Life of God in the Soul of Man* (Scotland, UK: Christian Focus Publications, 1996), 68.

"We both just turned fifty. Now all of a sudden he's got an insatiable ap-petite for sex. Our sex life had been good, I thought, but now his demands are totally insensitive. I like sex too, but sometimes—and more often now—I'm just not interested. Does God really expect me to be available to my husband for sex whenever he wants it? I just can't do it. I can't submit to him."

"I really want to marry this guy. But for three years, almost four, he's been telling me he's not ready. He says he loves me and he does treat me well. But we're both in our forties and never been married. I know I don't have to submit to him as if I were his wife. But I don't have a clue what submissive femininity would look like in this dating relationship, or even if it has a place. Am I supposed to just sweetly wait, tell him how wonderful he is, and pray that he makes his move?"

Two questions: What does each of these women think it means for a wife to submit to her husband? And what would you say to them? To the first question, the answer seems clear: do what you're told. That's what most of us think submission means. To the second question, I would guess that you, and most everyone else, might answer, "No. You shouldn't always submit. Some situations require that you not submit. Submitting to a man who is wrong would make you wrong."

There is a third question. When the Bible tells a wife to submit to her husband *in every way*—and that is what it says—what does it mean? How would God's Spirit, the real author of the Bible, prompt these women to respond to these men?

Well, you might say that's a question for scholars to wrestle with, not ordinary Christians without theology degrees. And yet even theologians can't always agree on the right answers to hard questions. Maybe the best thing to do when one of these women tells you her problem would be to trust your gut, honor whatever Christian principles come to mind, and offer advice that seems reasonable.

However, that demonstrates we don't trust the Bible, that we no longer depend on its teaching as both clear in its essentials and authoritative in everything. Without realizing (or admitting) it, I suspect a lot of Christians have done exactly that for three reasons:

1. *The Bible is hard to understand.* As I just mentioned, even serious Bible students don't always agree on important matters. What chance do we non-scholars have? If we don't know the culture into which

the "marriage passages" in Ephesians and 1 Peter were written, how are we going to understand what submission really means?

2. *The Bible can seem irrelevant to real life.* When relationships go sour, we need practical help. The Bible tells us that we need to know Jesus and do our best to follow Him, but when we need direct guidance, the Bible offers mostly general principles. We need specifics. What's an angry, confused wife to do? She needs real answers, not broad guidelines.

3. *The Bible takes us in directions we don't want to go.* God can be downright scary. We want Him to bless us with good things. He wants to form us, sometimes through hard things. We want to use the Bible to get the life we want and to use God to help us tell the story we want to tell with our lives. But the Bible wants us to fit the story of our lives into the story God is telling. God's story doesn't always line up too well with the story we want to tell.

It's true. The Bible can be hard to understand. It can seem irrelevant to the questions life makes us ask. And what it says sometimes does sound dangerous. Suffering doesn't appeal to us. We prefer blessings. But if we believe the Bible is literally God's Word, a correspondence of sixty-six love letters written by God to us, then giving up on the Bible, or skimming through it with little interest in studying it, are not options.

Two Convictions and Two Stories

As I wrestle with controversial topics such as what makes a woman feminine and what makes a man masculine, two core convictions keep me eagerly asking what the Bible means when it instructs women to submit to their husbands in everything:

1. Through God's Spirit, the Bible speaks loving and life-giving truth to men and women who genuinely long to live fully alive *in* God, fully alive *to* God, fully alive *with* God, and fully alive *for* God.

2. A biblically informed response in every situation is always available to people who want it, a response that accomplishes nothing less than revealing the beauty of God in even the ugliest of moments.

Those two convictions have kept this Christian psychologist somewhat sane for the past forty years. I've listened to story after story of heartbreak, disillusionment, lost faith, fury, and despair. Most of these stories revolve around dreams for relationships that were shattered, and all of them involve painful disappointment with life.

Here are two of them, both true stories that tested my convictions. Does God really speak loving and life-giving truth into difficult situations that provoke difficult questions? Does the Bible always inform a response to a difficult situation that brings joy to the responder?

Anne's Story

A woman named Anne scheduled an urgent appointment. Her husband of twenty years, a godly man she deeply respected, had just stunned her. Out of the blue, he told her that he wanted them to swap partners for an evening of sexual fun with a couple in their Bible study. The other couple had already agreed. Sobbing with anger, hurt, and confusion, this godly woman asked me, "What should I do? I've been submitting to my husband for twenty years. Am I supposed to submit to him now?"

Jean's Story

Jean and Alan had been married for three years. Both husband and wife were in their late twenties. Alan had asked Jean to cosign an application for a new car loan. When she looked over the papers Alan had already filled out, she realized that he had understated their outstanding debt and overstated their joint income. "I can't sign this. It's not honest," she said. Alan reminded her how badly he needed a new car. "You know my job has me on the road five days a week. And the old car I'm driving now is always breaking down and causing me to miss appointments. I'm losing money, every day. I really need you to cosign that application. I can't get the loan without your signature."

Jean had been raised in a Christian home. She wanted to be a good Christian wife. "Should I submit to my husband and sign the loan?" she asked. "Is that what God wants me to do?"

The Clean Truth

My impulse, and perhaps yours, would be to say, no, for God's sake don't submit. Don't have sex with another man. Don't sign a loan that's supported by false information. In these circumstances, a wife should not submit to her husband.

But resist that impulse and instead think biblically. What would it mean for these women to be a *suitable helper* for their husbands, to come alongside these weak, wrong men and provide strong help? Would a strong companion submit to either of these men? Paul told wives to submit to their husbands *in everything*. Did he mean what he said? Of course. But what did he mean?

How do most of us understand the word *submission*? When a husband tells his wife to join him in sexually swinging with another couple, the word *submission* sounds like a dirty word. And the way we think of it, it is.

But maybe the word needs a biblical bath, a spiritual scrubbing. Listen to God's Spirit speak through Peter to clean up the word. Let me repeat his inspired words with a few not-so-inspired comments of my own thrown in.

Likewise, wives, be subject [submit] to your own husbands, so that even if some do not obey the word [for example, arranging for immoral fun and lying on a loan application], they may be won [no guarantees; the goal is not to change the husband] without a word by the conduct of their wives [relational conduct—doesn't that involve words?], when they see your respectful and pure conduct. (1 Pet. 3:1–2)

Which means what, specifically?

Do not let your adorning [the way you present yourself as enticingly beautiful to your husband] be external—the braiding of hair and the putting on of gold jewelry, or the clothing you wear—but let your adorning [your enticing, soul-seducing beauty] be the hidden person of the heart with the imperishable beauty of a gentle and quiet spirit [two words with unexpected meaning; the spirit they describe is hidden in every Christian woman's heart, sometimes too hidden], which in God's sight is very precious. (vv. 3–4)

Why?

For this is how the holy women who hoped in God [holy because they knew their ultimate well-being depended on God, not their husbands; and their deepest affection was toward God, not their husbands] used to adorn themselves, by submitting to their husbands [submission, whatever it is, makes a woman beautiful? How?], as Sarah obeyed Abraham, calling him lord." [lord, not Lord, a term of respect, not worship] And you are her children, if you do good [like Sarah? When she didn't put up a fuss when Abraham offered her to a king for sex to save his own neck?] and do not fear anything that is frightening [be controlled not by what terrifies you, but by your love for God which frees you to be fully alive for Him in your femininity and to make God's beauty visible by the way you submissively relate]. (vv. 5–6)

Four observations in Peter's words that stand out to me can move us closer to a cleaned-up understanding of submission, and a liberating understanding of what makes a woman feminine.

Observation 1: Peter begins his discussion of submission with the word likewise.

In the previous chapter, Peter was talking about the crucifixion, where Jesus submitted to His Father by actively and freely choosing to yield to weak politicians and wicked soldiers. And now Peter says *likewise*? Is a woman to submit to God by yielding to ungodly husbands the way Jesus willingly yielded to ungodly men?

Yes. But don't jump to a disastrous conclusion! Peter is *not* telling wives to passively yield to abusive husbands. If your husband comes at you with a baseball bat, run to the nearest neighbor and call the police.

Remember our study of *neqebah*: a woman has been opened by God to receive *whatever advances His purposes*. Jesus was opened, as the Son who loved His Father, to do His Father's will. For Him, that meant Calvary. A godly wife is called to likewise submit like Jesus—whose primary purpose was to reveal His Father's heart and holiness.

I hear Peter telling women, *discern what you can do and say that most clearly reveals something beautiful about God that your husband needs to see, with the prayer that God will use your submission to further His will in your husband's life.* Don't be guided by what you most want your husband to do, or by what you most fear he might do, but rather by your openness to God to reveal what most represents the holy God of love.

Observation 2: The word translated submit *means "to arrange yourself under a larger design."*

Perhaps you're old enough to remember the Gomer Pyle television sitcom. Gomer was an uncoordinated, clumsy Marine who could never march in military formation. He walked the way his arrhythmic nature led him to walk. Each episode began with Sergeant Carter telling Private Pyle to *hypotassō*, to fall in line with the rhythm of the march.

Wives, *hypotassō*. That's the Greek word translated "submit" in 1 Peter 3:1. Don't mindlessly do what your husband tells you to do. There's a larger design to arrange yourself under, a larger and better story to tell. Submission requires wise discernment, not reflexive obedience. Ask this question: What action on your part tells—not the story you may prefer in the moment—but the eternal story God is telling, a profoundly good story with some deeply difficult chapters? Live to tell *that* story.

Watch out for a common mistake. A distraught wife may assume that marching in step with the Spirit's rhythm would never make her life more difficult. A wife who makes that assumption may refuse to be a suitably submissive helper, thinking she is telling God's story when she's telling her own story as she naturally prefers it to be told.

Observation 3: Submission is communicated more by attitude than action.

Peter speaks of a *gentle and quiet spirit* and seems to equate that spirit with the beauty a woman is opened to reveal. *Gentle* carries the idea of a solid center that no one can destroy. *Praus*, the Greek word translated "gentle," was also used to describe a once-wild horse that had been tamed, and came to mean "strength under control." A gentle woman relies on her inner strength to determine her actions, not her emotions that are triggered by how others treat her. A woman with a gentle spirit knows her husband has no power to destroy her beautiful soul, her feminine center. He can do great damage, but he can never destroy her identity as a woman made in God's image who is equipped to advance God's purpose.

A woman with a gentle spirit does not live in mortal fear of her husband. Fear no longer requires her to protect her soul. She is therefore free to honor a higher good, to respect her husband as a fellow image-bearer, and to invite him by her gentle attitude to be the man he was created to be.

A *quiet* spirit leads a woman to feel no controlling urge to "get even" with someone who has hurt her, to not return evil for evil. A woman with a quiet spirit may be outgoing or shy, opinionated or reserved, fun-loving and sociable or more serious and bookish. Whoever she is, her ruling passion is to invite the best from others by offering her best to others.

Years ago, Rachael and I left our two young boys with an older cousin while we traveled to Dallas. I had made it clear that something both boys wanted to do that weekend was not an option. In our hotel room Saturday afternoon, I was pacing the floor preparing for a difficult speech I was to give that evening.

When the phone rang, Rachael answered it. She listened for a minute, turned to me and said, "It's Kep. He thought of something that might persuade you to let them do what you had forbidden." She extended the phone toward me. Like a man on a mission, I said, "You handle it. I need to get ready for tonight."

Rachael looked at me warmly, said no, and placed the live phone close to me on the bed. Was she submitting to me? She was *open* to receiving whatever she discerned would further God's purposes in that moment, apparently deciding that encouraging me to put speaking ahead of fathering would not be good. She then *arranged her conduct* to fit in with her love for the story God was telling, a story that she wanted to tell with her life by inviting me to tell God's story with mine.

She knew I would be baffled, angry, and threatened by her strength. And I was all three. Yet whatever discomfort my reaction caused did not produce a fear that controlled her. With the *gentle* spirit of courageous and respectful love, she obeyed God, not me. And my dark mood after I again said no to my son did not generate scolding comments from her. She continued what she was doing before the phone call, reading, with a *quiet* spirit that felt no need to make me pay for my immaturity and unkindness.

Husbands, I might add, are not reliably or quickly drawn to a wife's cleaned-up submission.

Observation 4: Peter offers Sarah to women as an example of the beauty of submission.

Sarah? When did she respond to Abraham like Jesus, opened to receive whatever furthered God's will, arranging her action to fit in with God's larger story, uncontrolled by fear and with no impulse to respond to Abraham's weakness with anything but grace?

Peter lets us know that he is thinking of the one time in the Genesis story, Genesis 18, where Sarah called Abraham her master, her lord, indicating that she viewed him as worthy not of worship but of respect.

Years earlier, God had promised Abraham that he would be a father. Decades later, Sarah had not conceived. Perhaps she then remembered that God's promise made no specific mention she would be the mother. You know the story. Sarah then suggested that Abraham have sexual relations with Hagar, her servant girl. Ishmael arrived, and he was Abraham's son, but not the son of promise. God told Abraham to send both Hagar and Ishmael away.

More years passed. Abraham, now nearly a hundred years old, heard from God again. "You will be the father of a son *through Sarah*." Sarah, hiding in the tent, was eavesdropping. She heard that at age ninety she would finally become a mother. She laughed in disbelief. "Am I going to have this pleasure again with my master?" (see v. 12).

The pleasure she mentioned referred to sexual pleasure resulting in the joy of becoming a mother. By saying "again," she implied that she hadn't enjoyed sex with her hundred-year-old "master" for some time. And now, two old people would make love? A hundred-year-old man would successfully perform and a ninety-year-old woman would get pregnant? This must be some kind of joke.

Of course it wasn't. Notice that God's quite serious promise was doubly specific: a son would come through Sarah and the birth would take place in one year. Was God giving Abraham three months to work up his nerve? Even a man of faith struggles with doubt. In her earlier years, we're told, Sarah was a physically beautiful woman. In his earlier years, I imagine Abraham enjoyed an active sex life with his beautiful wife. But now?

See what happened. The man of faith made his move, I suspect three months later. The woman of imperishable beauty opened herself to receive her husband's God-honoring movement. Sarah submitted to God's purpose, as a woman fully alive in her femininity. And Peter says, "Wives, be like Sarah."

A woman once asked me if she should submit to a husband who wanted her to have sex with another man. I replied, "Of course. Submit in everything. Tell him no, gently and quietly."

Another woman asked me if she should cosign loan papers that she knew contained misinformation. Her husband wanted her to sign. Should she submit? I answered, "Yes. Submit in everything. Refuse to sign, gently and quietly."

If my response makes no sense, I believe it will by the time you read this whole book. If my response makes good sense now, by the time you finish this book it will make even better sense. It's making more sense to me every day.

There is much more to say about what makes a woman feminine as she relates, whether as a wife, girlfriend, sister, mother, daughter, or friend. But enough about women for now. It's time to turn our attention to men and ask the question: What makes a man *masculine*? Maybe that word needs a biblical bath too.

7

WHAT MAKES A MAN MASCULINE?

Men lust, but they know not what for: They fight and compete, but they forget the prize . . . they chase power and glory, but they miss the meaning of life.

George Gilder

Here I am in the twilight years of my life, still wondering what it is all about . . . I can tell you this, fame and fortune is for the birds.

Lee Iacocca

The true worth of a man is to be measured by the object he pursues.

Marcus Aurelius[1]

I hope I've been clear: this is not a book about husbands and wives. It is a book about men and women. Married or single, we all can live fully alive as either masculine men or feminine women. Marriage presents unique opportunities (and challenges) both for the physical and relational enjoyment of our gender and for our relational growth as gendered people. But the call to relate as masculine men or feminine women goes out to all of us, whether married, never married, divorced, or widowed.

1. Richard E. Simmons III, *The True Measure of a Man* (Mobile, AL: Evergreen Press, 2011), 18, 15, and 2, respectively.

A female person is feminine in God's eyes to the degree that she reveals God's relational nature by relating to others in two distinct ways: as an *opened* woman, opened to invite and receive movement from another that honors God, and as a *filled* woman, someone whose way of relating shows evidence that she gratefully receives the divine life that God pours into her and generously shares that life for the supreme purpose of nourishing God-honoring movement in others.

Let me say it more simply: like God, an opened woman invites godly movement and a filled woman nourishes godly movement. She owns no greater purpose. These few thoughts, including the ones on submission, only begin to tell the story of femininity. They raise a thousand questions.

But before we talk more about femininity, men (God help us) need equal time. Several women have suggested to me that men need *more* time!

Zakar

So God created human beings (*adam*) in his own image. In the image of God he created them; male (*zakar*) and female (*neqebah*) he created them. (Gen. 1:27 NLT)

I am *zakar,* whatever that means. Every male person is *zakar,* a man designed by God to reveal something about God by the way he relates, a male who can become masculine only by relating in a distinctly male way. But what is that way? What does *zakar* mean?

In Mark 10:6, Jesus uses the Greek word *arsen* to refer to a male person. On July 13, 1944, a doctor told my parents, "It's a boy." Had he spoken Hebrew and Greek, the doctor could have said, "Your baby is *zakar.* He is *arsen.*" A hospital chaplain who knew about such things might have added, "Your infant son was born to reveal something wonderful about God by the way he relates. Let the meaning of *zakar* and *arsen* guide you as you raise this boy to grow into a masculine man."

Can you imagine parents hearing those words and racing to find Hebrew and Greek dictionaries to discover what the chaplain was talking about? Of course not. Do we really need to study the meaning of *zakar* and *arsen* to understand what makes a male a man, a masculine man? Don't we already know?

If a man would simply stay moral and stay away from pornography, promiscuity, and perversion; if he commits to prioritizing family and friends above career success and employment stability; if he lives responsibly and honestly as he works hard; if he learns to communicate more and shut down less; if he does good things for the less fortunate with his time, talents, and money in his community and through his church, perhaps including an occasional mission trip to Africa, wouldn't that be enough? Wouldn't that male be a man?

Many good men think so. But that thinking misses the mark. It leaves good men shallow, prematurely content with themselves, and untroubled by something that should trouble them: *their inability to mirror God's penetrating and powerful love by moving deeply into another's soul with life-changing impact*. Such men are not only untroubled by their inability to powerfully love, they are unaware of this tragic inability. They have no comprehension of what the wise old priest Father Zosima meant when he said in Dostoyevsky's *The Brothers Karamazov*, "[Hell is] the suffering of being unable to love."[2]

Today's version of masculinity falls woefully short of God's design. A successful businessman who has no idea how to move deeply into his teenage daughter's soul is not masculine. Men today have little vision of what is possible for them if they would learn to relate with gospel power.

I've read a dozen books on what it means to be a man. Little thought is typically given to the dramatic truth that men bear the image of God, uniquely and differently than women. There seems to be little awareness that men, like women, were created by God to represent God by relating like God. Little excitement is generated by the idea that a man is called to enjoy God above every other pleasure, licit or illicit, by relating as men who relate like God.

When men devote their best energy to anything other than relating well in relational holiness, they may feel alive as men—but they are wrong. They are alive for themselves, not God. Only when a male lives out his designed destiny as a man does he become fully alive for the glory of God, as *zakar* and *arsen*.

Zakar means "to leave a mark, to make an impact." In ancient Near East culture, the word referred to a king's assistant, to a man charged with the important privilege of reminding the king of matters that required his

2. Fyodor Dostoyevsky, *The Brothers Karamazov* (Middlesex, England: Penguin, 1959), 312.

royal attention. *Zakar* came to mean someone who *remembers* something important that *moves* him to do something important.

If the idea of life-giving movement is implied by *zakar*, are we to think of a man's movement in the act of sex? We earlier discussed how *neqebah*, "opened," could refer to a woman's body as an image of the spiritual shape of a woman's soul. Perhaps *zakar* can also be interpreted beyond the physical: a man's movement in sex provides an image of how a masculine man moves in relationships.

Arsen

Arsen, Greek for *male*, means "to lift, to carry." It points to the strength needed to move something from one place to another. Together, *arsen* and *zakar* suggest the beginning idea that a man reflects God by remembering what is important and moving into a disordered situation with the strength to make an important difference. Now, as you continue reading, keep firmly in mind that a masculine man relates in a way that reflects something important about the way God relates, within the Trinity and with His people.

As they stand, these beginning thoughts make intuitive sense to a man. I feel good about myself when I remember something important that moves me with the strength I need to do something important. A surgeon remembers what he learned in his residency and deals competently with complications that arise in a delicate operation. An executive remembers his training in negotiation skills and effectively closes a big deal for his company. In the middle of a tense disagreement, a husband remembers a tip from a marriage seminar and takes his wife's hand, looks her gently in the eyes, and soothingly asks, "Please tell me exactly what you're feeling. I really want to know." And each of these men feels good about himself as a competent, effective, and sensitive man.

But each of these men falls short of God's idea of masculinity. Each has forgotten what supremely matters, and he leaves a mark that is less than the mark he was created to make. A less than profound relational understanding of what God wants men to remember, coupled with competent, effective, and sensitive movement that nevertheless accomplishes less than what men were designed to achieve, leaves men less than fully alive in their masculinity. They reveal less about God than God intended them to reveal. Unfortunately, such wrong thinking comes naturally to men. And it begins in boyhood.

I remember as an early teenager making a diving catch at third base, whirling quickly around, and throwing a perfect strike into the catcher's mitt. The catcher easily tagged out the base runner sliding into home. That out ended the game. We won, six to five. My teammates mobbed me. I was the *man*!

A few years later I took up fast-pitch softball, as a pitcher. I was good. My eighteen-year-old girlfriend (now my wife) sat high in the bleachers watching her eighteen-year-old boyfriend (me) perform. With blinding speed and effortless grace (at least that's how I choose to remember the moment), I delivered a pitch that blew past the hitter's flailing bat. Strike three! The final out. A victory in a big game. Again, my teammates mobbed me. But my eyes were riveted on a pretty brunette in a red and white checked dress jumping up and down, cheering for me. I was the *man*!

Less than a decade later, I graduated first in my PhD program in clinical psychology at the University of Illinois, leading the procession of fellow graduates across the stage in front of several thousand applauding parents, spouses, friends, and children. Not long afterward, I was preaching in a church with Pat Zondervan, the founder of Zondervan Publishing, in attendance. He approached me to say that he heard a book in my message and would be open to receiving a manuscript from me. Within a few years, my name—*Dr. Crabb*—gained wide recognition in the Christian world. To God be the glory. Great was His faithfulness. I was alive with talent and success, leaving my mark. I was the *man*! And I liked the feeling.

As someone put it, my path to counterfeit masculinity began on the ball field, shifted to the bedroom, and moved into the boardroom.

Meanwhile, my marriage was crumbling. Rachael felt unseen; her soul was invisible to me as I chased after my first love. Physical adultery? No. Something worse: spiritual adultery. The god I was revealing to my wife was the god of this world, even as I preached in churches and wrote Christian books. I had forgotten the kind of movement that mattered most. I had moved away from God, and from my wife and two little boys, to chase after what I remembered would help me feel good about myself—displayed talent, pleasurable lust, and recognized success.

I was not moving as a man across the bridge to pour sacrificing love into an opened woman, or into anyone else. To borrow a phrase from

Augustine, I was curved in on myself, forgetting the God whose image I bore, deaf to His call to enjoy Him by revealing His humble love for me by humbly loving others.

I was moving, but not across the Bridge of Connection. I was moving into myself as a demanding narcissist. I was a success, but I was not masculine.

I see now—I didn't see it then—that my relational paralysis was relational sin. No drunkenness, no pornography, no laziness, no dishonesty—only a way of relating that revealed a wrong god and left my wife opened and unentered, her feminine soul unseen and untouched. I was *not* the man! And I was making it difficult for my wife to remain open, to invite godly movement from a man who had no understanding of what godly movement was. But I thought I did. I was content in my spiritual immaturity—for far too long a season.

Until a man mirrors, however stumblingly, the relational movement of the God who never forgets His covenant and never stops moving in costly love, that man will never know what it means to be fully alive in his masculinity for the glory of God.

Until a man's movement toward others reveals God's movement toward him, until a man remembers that he bears God's image and moves to reveal God's character to others, that man will pursue counterfeit masculinity with the fierce loyalty of an addict, whether through displayed talent, pleasurable lust, or recognized success.

—

Zakar: a man who never forgets that he bears God's image, that nothing matters more than bringing Christ's kingdom to earth by crossing the bridge to strongly enter the lives of others with divine weight.

Arsen: a man who knows that he will never move well into others until he is broken by how obsessed he is with his own well-being and cries mercy as he seeks God with all his heart. This man knows that without God's life energizing his movement he will remain stuck on his end of the bridge, weak, unable to love, and deeply impacting no one with God's life.

Questions remain. What would it look like for a God-remembering, God-dependent man to move in God-revealing ways toward a wife who has closed herself, toward a son or daughter who is breaking his heart, toward parents who have failed him, toward a once-close friend who has turned against him, toward a colleague who he realizes has been backstabbing him to advance his or her own position in the company?

And what would it look like for a masculine man to move toward a responsive wife, great kids, faithful parents, still-close friends, and supportive colleagues?

Two passages, one in Genesis, the other in Exodus, provide beginning hints of what it means to live as a man fully alive in his masculinity for the glory of God, a man who seizes the relational opportunity when he sees—really *sees*—the person standing on the other end of the bridge.

8

RELATIONAL MASCULINITY

If you limit your choices only to what seems reasonable or possible, you disconnect yourself from what you truly want. And all that's left is a compromise.

Robert Fritz[1]

The resurrection is . . . the symbol and pledge of a humanity reaching its proper goal, where the "sin" story of human life in Adam is overtaken and consumed by the "grace" story told in Christ.

Brendon Byrne[2]

The task of the new humanity is to show forth in conduct the ways of God.

Stanley J. Grenz[3]

All human community is centered around the community of men and women.

Claus Westermann[4]

Before I say more about what makes a male a man, notice the rhythm of thought that flows through these four quotes. It's a rhythm that, once

1. Robert Fritz, *By the Path of Least Resistance* (New York: Random House, 1986).
2. Stanley J. Grenz, *The Social God and the Relational Self* (Louisville, KY: Westminster John Knox Press, 2001), 224.
3. Ibid., 263.
4. Ibid., 272.

caught, can carry us into the confident hope that we really can live as fully alive men and women for the glory of God.

- Quote 1: Pursue a vision for yourself that seems unreasonable, a vision that is within reach only if you connect with a desire within your soul that will never be satisfied without outside help.
- Quote 2: Thanks to the "grace" story, outside help is available that, when accepted, becomes inside help. We *will* connect with what we truly want, with our buried desire to reveal God to others by the way we relate. We *will* overcome the "sin" story of counterfeit masculinity and femininity. We *will* become fully alive as male and female image-bearers. And in true community, when we meet on the bridge, we *will* enjoy perfect harmony, complete satisfaction, exhilarating wholeness, and sheer delight as masculine men and feminine women. It *will* happen, in measure now and in fullness forever.
- Quote 3: It is our God-guaranteed destiny to relate with each other in the enjoyment of God. It can happen. It *will* happen.
- Quote 4: Divorce, abandonment, rejection, inadequacy, awkwardness, loneliness, insignificance, failure—everything that keeps us from meeting on the bridge—will become things of the past, gladly forgotten. For now, we can journey through relational suffering toward the seemingly impossible dream of our relational destiny, a dream that, when it becomes our strongest ambition and our most resolute aim, will never again be shattered. As we journey on a narrow road, we will learn to dance together as men and women who provide a taste of heaven's community, a taste that will become an eternal, overflowing banquet.

Think of what the grace story reveals about our social God. God's way of relating is invitational, opened wide to welcome all who come to His party and fully supplied to provide the nourishment we need to learn the Trinitarian dance. *Relational femininity reveals the invitational beauty of God.*

And God's way of relating is incarnational, always remembering His covenantal resolve to have us with Him, and sacrificially moving into our lostness all the way to the cross in order to bring us to Him. *Relational masculinity reveals the incarnational beauty of God.*

Let me now offer a few more beginning thoughts on masculinity, first from Genesis, then from Exodus. I want us to see what it looks like for men to reveal God as they move into their everyday relationships.

Adam's Opportunity to Be a Man, Seized Then Missed

The first chapter of Genesis, along with the first three verses of chapter 2, paints a "big picture" view of creation by a uniquely powerful, transcendent God. Following Genesis 2:4, the text zeroes in on God's creation of Adam and Eve, and tells us things we weren't told in chapter 1.

God only hinted at His relational nature in Genesis 1:26 when He said, "Let us make human beings in our image." But in chapter 2, we clearly see that God is not only *above* us in transcendent majesty, He is also *with us* in immanent love, as a happy, social God whose plan is to include us in the joy of His community.

But God's warm invitation to dance with Him is accompanied by a firm warning: we must never believe the lie that God would withhold any good thing from us. We must never chase after anything He forbids, thinking we'll enjoy more goodness than He provides. We must trust God to define what is good by what He provides or allows, and trust Him to define what is bad by what He forbids or withholds. (There are times, of course, when God withholds good things for our greater good.)

Then, notice the command not to eat from a certain tree (a command that presents the opportunity to celebrate God's provision by honoring His prohibition [Gen. 2:16–17]) is immediately followed by God's observation that "it is not good that the man should be alone," and by His declared intent to make further provision for Adam, "I will make him a helper fit for him" (v. 18).

Notice two things about this strange sequence of warning then blessing. First, *God followed His prohibition by increasing His provision.* God created Eve so that the man and woman could dance together in the rhythm of His love and so put His relational glory on display. He provided everything we needed to share in the joy of the Trinity's party. As C. S. Lewis insightfully wrote, "Joy is the serious business of heaven."[5]

We need to be clear: God's prohibitions exist to safeguard the enjoyment of His provisions. God told Adam what not to do so that he and his soon-to-arrive wife would enjoy all that they could do.

Second, perhaps stranger than the first: *God issued His warning to Adam before Eve was created.* Why? God was giving Adam an opportunity to

5. C. S. Lewis, *Letters to Malcolm: Chiefly on Prayer* (New York: Harcourt, 1964), 93.

remember and move, to relate as a man by remembering something important and by moving to accomplish something important. The Genesis story clearly implies that Adam was to tell Eve what he remembered God had said, and that he did so.

When? In chapter 1, we see God blessing *both* Adam and Eve (see vv. 28–30). But in chapter 2, we see God warning only Adam before Eve was created. The chapter 1 blessing came *after* the chapter 2 warning. The sequence is clear: God warned Adam not to eat the forbidden fruit; He then created Eve, and later blessed them both.

After they receive God's blessing, I picture Adam and Eve walking happily hand in hand through the paradise of God's provision, marveling over how lavishly God had blessed them, literally having the time of their lives. Perhaps it was during that walk that Adam pointed to one particular tree and told Eve of God's warning. I presume he repeated what he remembered word for word. We don't know for sure, of course, *when* Adam remembered and moved. *That* he remembered and moved is certain.

It was the man's first opportunity to enjoy relational masculinity, and he seized it. I imagine Eve attentively and appreciatively listening as Adam spoke protectively, with her best interests in mind. I see them meeting on the bridge when Adam remembered and moved toward his opened and nourishing wife.

A second opportunity for Adam to practice relational masculinity comes in chapter 3, when a devil-inspired snake engaged Eve in a fateful conversation, fogging her memory of the warning from God that she had heard from her husband. Eve was standing on her end of the bridge, naively open to Satan's cunning deceit. Adam was listening to the conversation from his end of the bridge. It was the perfect opportunity for Adam to again remember and move, to cross the bridge and speak to Eve.

"Honey, don't listen to the snake. Listen to God. Let me tell you again exactly what I remember He said. God did not say that we couldn't *touch* the tree. You're highlighting His prohibition more than His provision. And if I heard you right, you seemed to imply that if we ate the forbidden fruit we *might* die. God said we would *surely* die. You're minimizing the certainty of terrible consequences for disobedience."

But Adam remained silent. He failed to remember and move. That first failure of relational masculinity has now become the pattern of relating that comes naturally to all Adam's male descendants. Men don't cross the bridge. Husbands shut down. They turn away from moving with protective strength into their wives' desire for intimacy. Men make only those choices that seem reasonable and possible. They enjoy counterfeit masculinity, masculine pleasure without relationally masculine movement. They look at pornography, live for recognized success, and lust after feelings of significance and adequacy through any means that require little relational risk.

In His infinite patience, God never stops calling men to remember who He is, how He relates, and what He teaches, and then to move toward others, to relate with one uncompromised purpose: *to reveal what they remember.* Men who hear God's call and then remember and move become masculine men. All others do not.

Movement Always Follows Remembering

When God remembers, He moves—always. He acts to restore whatever good was lost, and He provides for the well-being of His people. The Bible makes that clear (emphasis in verses mine).

1. "God *remembered* Noah . . . and the waters subsided . . . Then God said to Noah, 'Go out from the ark . . . and be fruitful'" (Gen. 8:1, 15–17).
2. "God *remembered* Abraham and sent Lot out of the midst of the overthrow when he overthrew the cities in which Lot had lived" (Gen. 19:29).
3. "Then God *remembered* Rachel, and God . . . opened her womb" (Gen. 30:22).
4. "[Israel's] cry for rescue came up to God. And God heard their groaning, and God *remembered* his covenant . . . God saw the people of Israel—and God knew" (Exod. 2:23–25).
5. Moses implored God, "*Remember* . . . your servants to whom you swore by your own self, and said to them, 'I will multiply your offspring . . . and all this land that I have promised I will give to your offspring, and they shall inherit it forever'. And the LORD relented from the disaster that he had spoken of bringing on his people" (Exod. 32:13–14).
6. "*Remember* your mercy, O LORD, and your steadfast love . . . *Remember* not the sins of my youth . . . according to your steadfast

love *remember* me, for the sake of your goodness, O LORD!" (Ps. 25:6–7).

7. "O God, why do you cast us off forever? . . . *Remember* your congregation . . . which you have redeemed! . . . *Remember* Mt. Zion where you have dwelt" (Ps. 74:1–2).

When God remembers, He moves. And God's people knew that was how He related. When they were in trouble, they pleaded with God to remember His character and covenant, knowing that when He remembered, He would move on their behalf.

Look more closely at Exodus 2:23–25. In the New Living Translation, it reads like this:

> The Israelites continued to groan under their burden of slavery. They cried out for help, and their cry rose up to God. God heard their groaning, and he remembered his covenant promise to Abraham, Isaac, and Jacob. He looked down on the people of Israel and knew it was time to act.

An alternate translation of that last phrase reads "and acknowledged his obligation to help them."

Notice what God did in this passage: He *heard*, He *remembered*, He *looked*, and He *acted*. Whatever else might legitimately be involved in a man's relating with a wife, child, parent, friend, girlfriend, or colleague, if he is to be relationally masculine he will hear, remember, look, and act.

- *A masculine man hears the cry of others.* A cry is rising up in every human heart: from unmet longings, shattered dreams, deep fears, or repeated failures. In seasons of blessing, the cry might be muffled, even to the one who cries. But a masculine man is always listening. No matter how intense his own cry may be, he hears the cry of another, just as Jesus heard His mother's anguish while He was nailed to a cross.

- *A masculine man remembers the God he is called to reveal.* He remembers whose image he bears, whose purpose he lives to advance, whose call he longs to follow. He may feel criticized by his wife, disappointed by his children, unappreciated by his parents, betrayed by his friends, backstabbed by his colleagues, terrified at the prospect of business failure, or empty and weak. He may hurt deeply, but he remembers his God. And he knows he is here to reveal God's faithful, forgiving, forever love to others.

- A *masculine man looks into another's distress and feels his own inadequacy that only God can overcome.* He is more curious than immediately helpful. He refuses to offer quick advice or easy solutions, the kind of help that he is comfortable offering. Rather than attempting to manage someone's problem, he looks at the problem until he feels inadequate to solve it, and realizes the best he can do is to offer the presence of Christ by the way he is with another.

- A *masculine man moves into another's need in order to reveal God's holy heart of love.* He knows it is time to act when he hears someone's cry, remembers the story of God that he longs to tell with his life, and looks carefully to discern God's timely provision for someone's real (perhaps unfelt) need. He is willing to leave his comfort zone, to move without feeling adequate, and to take the risk that another may not appreciate his movement. He trusts what he prayerfully discerns is deepest within him as he hears, remembers, and looks. He moves gently but decisively into another person's life, entering through whatever relational opening is provided by another's need. His joy depends not on another's appreciation but on the privilege of representing the God whose image he bears, by the way he relates to others.

If relational femininity is displayed in a woman who is opened to receive godly movement and longs to nourish godly movement, relational masculinity is revealed in a man who remembers God's story and moves to advance its plot. If we catch even a dim vision of the high calling of God on our lives, we will wake up from our long nap with sweet desire. We will *want* to live fully alive as feminine women and masculine men.

What keeps us from indulging our deepest desire to be fully alive as feminine women and masculine men who reveal by the way we relate the beauty of the way God relates? I'll answer that question in Part II.

Hint: whether we know it or not, whether we feel it or not, we're all literally scared to death.

DISCOVERING OUR CORE TERROR

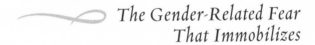 *The Gender-Related Fear
That Immobilizes*

As fallen image-bearers, we are both *reliant on God* for living as fully alive men and women and *hostile to God*, angrily determined to enjoy our gendered existence without depending on God for personal wholeness and relational satisfaction. Rejected dependence on God and unchallenged hostility to God results in a core terror that our longing to live fully as men and women will never be realized, and that we will remain personally empty and relationally disconnected. Willful denial of this terror, coupled with the stubborn belief that we control how our deepest longings can be satisfied, defines what the Bible calls foolishness—an arrogant independence that seems wise for a season but will be exposed as existential stupidity.

> Sin is the destruction of community. . . . Rather than enjoying the presence of God, we flee. We live in fear, presuming that God is hostile toward us, although we are in fact the hostile ones and project our hostility on God.

Despite our infinite dependence, we run from the only one who can over-come our fear, brokenness, and hostility, the one who can fulfill our deepest needs. Sin, therefore, destroys the community God intends for his creation . . . Consequently, we are alienated from our own true selves. We simply are not who we are meant to be.

Stanley J. Grenz[1]

In Part II we'll discover the core terror that lives in the heart of a woman and a man. The fear that justifies self-protective relating, even though often denied and unfelt, still has the power to keep us from revealing God by relating as feminine or masculine image-bearers. Worse, it can keep us from discovering our desire to do so.

1. Stanley J. Grenz, *Theology for the Community of God* (Grand Rapids: Eerdmans, 2000), 187, 208.

9

WE HAVE NOTHING TO FEAR EXCEPT . . .

Because God's children are human beings—made of flesh and blood—the Son also became flesh and blood. For only as a human being could he die, and only by dying could he break the power of the devil, who had the power of death. Only in this way could he set free all who have lived their lives as slaves to the fear of dying.

Hebrews 2:14–15 NLT

And they heard the sound of the LORD God walking in the garden in the cool of the day, and the man and his wife hid themselves from the presence of the LORD God among the trees of the garden. But the LORD God called to the man and said to him, "Where are you?" And he said, "I heard the sound of you in the garden, and I was afraid, because I was naked, and I hid myself."

Genesis 3:8–10

The above two passages can help us begin to understand why most of us don't live fully alive in either our femininity or masculinity. Notice:

- The devil, working through the world and in our flesh, blinds us to the unique joy of revealing God to others by the way we relate. He keeps us worried by the fear that we will never know the deep delights of fully alive womanhood or manhood. He persuades us that it is good and right to do whatever it takes to protect ourselves from our worst fears and to feel as good about ourselves as we can, at any cost to others.

- Fear is the first human emotion specifically mentioned in the Bible. It's the first and strongest emotion felt after Adam and Eve took it on themselves to arrange for their maximum enjoyment of life. That insubordinate arrogance has been passed on to all their descendants— to you and me. We now assume responsibility in managing our joy. To manage what cannot be managed risks inevitable failure, which generates fear. Until we allow God to accomplish His deepest work in us, the fear that our souls will never really live shapes and energizes the way we relate to each other. When fear functions as our ruling passion, self-protective, self-centered relating feels necessary and natural. It's how we relate when we live "as slaves to the fear of dying" (Heb. 2:15 NLT).

- When protecting ourselves from the pain that others can cause us becomes our justified priority, unrecognized as evil and therefore never meaningfully confessed, the presence of God is not welcomed. It is avoided. Without confessed brokenness over relational sin, any loving experience of the relationally holy God is counterfeit. Relational holiness enrages us by exposing the wrongness of the relational sin that we cling to for survival. Until the wonder of grace amazes us, the fear of God's rejection won't draw us to Him.

- The masks we wear, the fig leaves we clothe ourselves with, the personas we present to others to make sure they never have reasonable grounds to criticize or reject us, and the secrets we keep to preserve a favorable social image—they're all designed to keep a terrible fear at bay and to numb the pain of impending soul-death that threatens to destroy us. They keep us alone, feeling unwanted and disrespected as we go about our lives.

- With our masks, fig leaves, personas, and secrets all well-positioned, we live not to reveal the God of love by the way we relate, but to hide from the fear that threatens to destroy us—our core terror. The result? We fall short of God's relational glory. We are never fully alive in relational femininity or masculinity. We live alone, in silent misery, meeting no one on the bridge.

Perhaps a story, what I call "The Parable of the Uncrossed Bridge," might help to put us in touch with the core terror in our souls that has the power to keep us in slavery to the fear of death, a fear that seems to justify self-centered relating and blinds us to the high and joyful calling of God, to the glory-filled vision of living fully alive in relational femininity or masculinity.

The Parable of the Uncrossed Bridge

The First Dreamer

A woman's pastor said there was no such thing as hell. The woman disagreed. She was already there.

"Could any hell be worse than the one I live in every day?" she wondered.

Her loneliness was unbearable. Her fear paralyzed her.

"If there is a worse hell," she mused, "it must be a place where no distractions from suffering are available, where no relationship provides even the illusion of intimacy, where no fleeting moments of fun relieve the pain, and where it's impossible to believe that anything you do matters, because it doesn't."

Although she lived alone in her private hell, the woman managed to function. She was really quite resourceful. She was somehow able to crawl out of her dark dungeon into the world of people and socialize. Some days she could engage with her job as though it were important. And she could laugh. She could be amused by a clever movie, find pleasure at a lively party, and feel a trickle of hope that her life could even be satisfying when she read a well-written novel about lost love regained.

The woman could manage her life; it was her soul she couldn't deal with. As long as she kept emotional distance from the unnamed pain that was always there, she could survive. For brief seasons, she could even think she was thriving. Almost.

But thinking was hard. It forced her to admit that one goal directed her choices, that one desperate passion provided energy for its pursuit. In a moment of uncomfortable insight, the woman wrote these words in her rarely used journal: "I must keep the fog of nothingness that fills my soul from destroying whatever happiness I can manage to produce."

She had no lack of friends; men and women sincerely enjoyed her. She was witty, intelligent, attractive, and usually ready to do fun things. Of course people enjoyed her. But she wanted more. She longed to be explored, seen, and wanted, even in her struggles and failures. But the woman was afraid. So she presented herself as having it all together. Her friends bought the lie. They never fought to enter her soul. They related with whom she pretended to be, thinking they were meeting her, believing their friendship was deep.

The woman felt like an imposter, projecting an image to others while living in unseen misery. Others enjoyed her lively personality, her willingness to help when needed, her many talents that made her a competent woman. But a question that she asked no one but herself was troubling: "Do I present these virtues to others the way a well-shaped mannequin displays fashions to those who pass by, those who pause to look and then move on?"

She tried not to think about such things. Thinking made it difficult to preserve the illusion that she was successfully managing her life, that she was content. Thinking made it hard to pretend. And it was pretending that made her life bearable.

Until nighttime.

She couldn't remember when the dream began. Perhaps it began when she was a little girl, when night terrors first visited her sleep. If that was so, the dream must have appeared on the screen of her young mind like a fuzzy picture on an old television set with those rabbit ears antennae that no one could properly adjust.

But now the dream came in high definition, several nights every week, so vivid and clear that it seemed more real than reality. Perhaps it was. Perhaps her dream was reality, and her life was a dream—not an especially good one, but at least an escape from the hellish reality exposed in her dream. The thought made her shudder.

It was always the same, a long, narrow bridge stretching between two jagged edges of a cliff over a mile-deep chasm; a bridge with no guardrails, clearly a dangerous bridge to cross. Falling meant certain death.

In the dream, the woman always saw herself standing on the cliff edge at one end of the bridge. A man, faceless except for eyes that were fastened on her, stood at the other end of the bridge.

The woman did not want to move. Falling was a terrifying possibility. But there was another reason she didn't want to move, a strange but stronger reason. Moving across the bridge just didn't seem right. It felt like putting size five shoes on size seven feet. Moving didn't fit her soul. The man should move. That somehow felt better, the way things were supposed to be.

Was she just old-fashioned, wanting to still live in a day when men opened doors for women? *That's silly*, she told herself. *I can open a door for myself perfectly well. But I can't stop hoping the man will cross the bridge to be with me. Is that silly too?* She wasn't sure.

The man didn't move. She could see desire in his eyes, desire for her, desire to move and be with her. Perhaps if she waited on her side of the bridge with arms opened wide to invite him, he would move.

But she also saw fear in his eyes. The fear, even from her distance on the far side of the bridge, seemed stronger to her than his desire. "Why is he so afraid? Do I somehow seem dangerous to him?"

The woman waited. But then she watched herself move. Throwing caution into the winds of desire, she ran across the long, narrow bridge toward the man on the other side.

"Can't you see me? I'm coming to you. I want to be with you. I want you to want me. Open your arms to receive me. Please. I can't bear to live alone, to be alone, without a man who loves me."

But sometimes in her dream, as she moved, she noticed something troubling. The fear in the man's eyes turned into anger. His desire disappeared. Her movement made him uncomfortable, even resentful. Why? She didn't understand.

Confusion then turned her desire into fear. "He doesn't want me. There is nothing to want. I'm nothing. Singleness is my prison cell, my isolation from life."

And then she looked down. She lost her balance and fell. And as she fell, the dream ended. She woke up shaking with fear, sobbing in despair as she descended into the fog of nothingness that defined who she was. She disappeared.

Mercifully, the dream more often had a different ending. When she had moved halfway across the bridge, she would see in the man's eyes more stubbornness than fear. And that would make her mad.

"Why would I want such a selfish, stubborn, weak man? I'll just turn around, get back to the safety of my managed life, work hard, hang out with my friends, and see a good movie. My friends don't really know me. But that's okay. And the single life is safe. And I can make it work."

With that decision, she would wake up feeling sad and resigned, but determined to move on with her life.

Either way, whether the dream left her disappearing or determined, the woman was nearer to death than life. She was alone, invisible in a world full of people. She had no vision of what it would mean to be fully alive as a woman, to be *feminine*, married or single.

The Second Dreamer

The man thought he enjoyed church. He thought he believed what the pastor said. He thought he was a decent guy, a good Christian man, especially when he wrote sizable checks to his church, an amount slightly above the commanded tithe of his substantial income. The man had no idea that he was self-righteous, self-centered, shallow—and scared.

A strong dread was always present somewhere inside him. But he managed to smother it beneath overwork, a good sense of humor, and consistent scores in the low eighties on the golf course—occasionally even in the seventies. The dread, whatever it was, remained mostly unfelt and stubbornly unexamined.

But something kept bothering him. *Why can't I get that sentence out of my mind?* he asked himself. Not much that the pastor said stayed with him past the closing prayer. But one sentence had. He could quote it verbatim, and he did, to himself, quite often.

> Most men are driven by a hidden fear, by a fear of losing what they wrongly believe is essential to the enjoyment of their true manhood.

True manhood? What's he talking about? The man felt more irritated than intrigued by the question.

He read mostly action novels and business books and scanned the *Wall Street Journal* every day. But a friend had recently given him a book about masculinity and said it was a must-read eye-opener.

The opening sentence in the introduction, a long one—too long he thought—stuck with him, like that one sentence from his pastor. He didn't know why. But he did something he had never done before. He wrote it down on a small index card and kept it folded in his wallet. He read it at least once a week.

> If you're given to outbursts of rage that you later regret, if sexual urges drive you toward satisfaction with little thought of anyone but yourself, if your conversations with men revolve mostly around business, sports, politics, and social banter, if moving toward your wife or girlfriend to help her be fully alive as a woman is a new thought, if even one of these things is true in your life, then you're likely living with a false understanding of what it means to be a man.

Both sentences unsettled the man, but he remained incurious and un-convicted. Well, maybe he was a little curious. *Am I missing something? Do I have a false understanding of what it means to be a man?*

But given another long drive down the middle of the fairway, another sexual fantasy indulged, another good time with friends, another signed contract that guaranteed big money and allowed him to write an even bigger check to the church—he felt fine.

The discomfort of a vague and unnamed dread and the unsettling ques-tions provoked by those two sentences gave way to the pleasures of recog-nized competence, enjoyable relationships, visible achievement, and felt significance. Add to that the added bonus of a swaggering sense of personal wholeness, tied in with the belief that his many blessings represented God's favor, and life was good.

Until nighttime.

When he turned off the television and the light on his nightstand, the man strangely felt like the little boy who pulled the covers over his neck so Dracula couldn't bite him, the scared kid who wouldn't let his arms drop down toward the floor in order to keep the crocodile hiding under the bed from chomping them off, the terrified child begging God to protect him from the boogeyman in the closet who might come out and kill him. He was suddenly all of that, but now in adult form.

Was the man now afraid that *life* would bite him? Had the arm chomp-ing crocodile morphed into an uncertain career, relationships that were fun and useful but not deep, or inevitable health problems? Could the boogeyman now be inside him, threatening to somehow destroy every-thing he had?

And that dream, that dream that plagued his sleep and left him unnerved every time. What was that about?

It was always the same, a long, narrow bridge stretching between two jagged edges of a cliff over a mile-deep chasm; a bridge with no guardrails, clearly a dangerous bridge to cross. Falling meant certain death.

In the dream, he always saw a man standing on the cliff edge at one end of the bridge. A woman, faceless except for eyes that were riveted on him, stood at the other end of the bridge.

He knew he was the man in the dream. And he knew that he wanted to move, to cross the bridge to meet the woman. Moving felt right, like putting size 10 shoes on size 10 feet.

Her eyes invited him. But he wouldn't move. Even in his dream, he was puzzled. *Why won't I move?* he asked himself. *I know crossing the bridge is dangerous. And I am afraid of falling. But there's something more holding me back. I don't know what it is. I want to be with her, to be for her, to be in her. But I won't move. I don't know why.*

One thing seemed clear: he was more immobilized by the fear of some sort of failure or criticism than motivated by the hope of intimacy, yet it was an intimacy he deeply wanted. As he continued to stand there, the woman moved. She stepped onto the bridge—aggressively, he thought. She was coming toward him, still far away, but closer every second.

The man's confusion suddenly became rage. *Does she think I can't move? Of course I can. Maybe I don't want to move toward this woman. Why won't she go back to her side of the bridge and wait for me to move? Oh, I know why. She disrespects me. She thinks I'm weak. Well, I'm not going to disrespect myself by receiving her movement like a scared little boy receiving his mother's comforting kiss. Relationships are such a hassle. Useful colleagues and fun friends are so much easier.*

The man no longer felt as drawn by the desire he saw in the woman's eyes. He was now irritated by her movement.

And he was surprised by what he sometimes did next in the dream. He stepped onto the bridge, a small step followed by slow movement. He still wanted to connect with the woman. But the nearer he came to her, the more that damnable dread overwhelmed his desire. And the more mad and stubborn he felt.

Then he looked down, lost his balance, and fell off the bridge.

At that moment he would wake up, sweating, shaken to the core, eager to grab his clubs and head to the golf course, tempted to indulge his most satisfying sexual fantasy, ready to start planning his next business deal. The thought of speaking with someone at church never crossed his mind. *Why? What does church have to do with anything really important to me?*

More often, however, the dream ended differently. He never moved. The woman stopped moving toward him, looked into his eyes, shrugged her shoulders, turned around, and returned to her side of the bridge.

He hated her for moving toward him. He hated her more for moving away from him.

Most women would be thrilled to live with him. He had it all: charm, money, good looks, decent morals, a good sense of humor, an important job, and lots of sexual energy. He was a decent guy, a good Christian man. What was her problem? The single life, with its serial dating and sexual hookups, was sounding pretty good.

It occurred to him, still in his dream, that maybe he'd stay sexually pure. No sex. At least not too often. That would be more "Christian."

And then he would wake up, more self-righteous, more self-centered, and more shallow than before, and even more convinced that he was a decent guy, a good Christian man. And really quite masculine.

He'd forget the dream and get on with his day, wondering about marriage, occasionally thinking it could be a good thing. But he couldn't quite forget those two sentences. The dread they provoked remained with him, like a nagging headache, and stole some of the joy he felt when he hit a great drive with a couple of buddies watching, or mentally undressed an attractive woman, or scheduled a big closing.

The man was nearer to death than life. He was alone, terrified that his movement would make no difference, but willfully unaware of his fear. He had no vision of what it would mean to be fully alive as a man, to be *masculine*, married or single.

An unfeminine woman and an unmasculine man will always live at a distance from each other and from their friends. They will never connect. Pleasant times and passionate feelings might mimic connection, but real connection never happens, either in marriage or friendships.

But when a woman is feminine and a man is masculine, community happens. People meet—on the bridge. And God is revealed.

What are these core terrors that keep men and women from living fully alive for the glory of God?

10

The Core Terror of a Woman

An Invitation with No Response

Come to me . . . and I will give you rest.

Jesus (Matt. 11:28)

O Jerusalem, Jerusalem. . . . How often I have wanted to gather your children together as a hen protects her chicks beneath her wings, but you wouldn't let me.

Jesus (Matt. 23:37 NLT)

[He had] no beauty that we should desire him.

Isaiah 53:2

There is no fear in love, but perfect love casts out fear. . . . Whoever fears has not been perfected in love.

1 John 4:18

Relational femininity carries with it a terrible risk. When a woman relates to others with Christ's invitational beauty, opened to welcome rather than closed to protect, and available to nourish rather than positioned to get, she risks losing everything she values; well, everything except God.

If you can envision no greater good than knowing God Himself, if the phrase "Jesus plus nothing is everything" rings true in your heart as more than a cute and inspiring cliché, and if you accept that knowing God personally, in the depths of intimacy with which He can be known, empowers you to reveal Him relationally in a way that brings you into fellowship with His suffering, then you will hear the Spirit whisper these words in your soul:

> Pursue your greatest good with a passion that will weaken your resolve to avoid your worst fear. Don't live to avoid what you most fear. Live to gain what you most want. Only then will you discover whom Jesus has made you: a beautiful woman in whom the Father delights, a powerful woman whom God can use to bring His kingdom to earth.

But there's a catch, a big one: first, you must die to the power of the devil in order to be free from slavery to your deepest fears. You must confront your core terror. To live alive as a woman, free to be all that you are, you must take the risk of relational femininity. The risk is real.

- A man may refuse to enter the opened heart of a beautifully feminine woman. With the blindness that afflicts so many men, he may see no beauty in her soul that entices him to a lifelong commitment.
- A husband already committed by sacred vows may sinfully turn away from an opened and nourishing wife, finding a more easily enjoyed satisfaction in career success, ministry achievements, pornographic pleasures, or even spiritual disciplines.
- A Christian man who wants to be a good dad may not recognize his lack of meaningful involvement with his daughter. Touching her soul with the masculine power of a father's love may seem to him intimidating, awkward, and confusing. Watching television is more relaxing. His daughter gets the message: she has no beauty worth fighting for.
- Friends, both men and women, may be warmly attracted to the company of a deeply godly woman without it ever occurring to them to explore her depths. She gets the message: she has an engaging personality and is usefully talented, and nothing more. There is no compelling

beauty visible to others that lies within her, waiting to be discovered and celebrated.

Inviting, and no one comes. Opened, and unentered. Nourishing, and people go elsewhere. Relational femininity is risky. A devastating conclusion seems unavoidable: *relating as a feminine woman is a stupid attempt to reveal beauty that does not exist*. The possible result is too painful to bear.

What woman in her right mind would take that risk in such a relationally uncertain and dangerous world? Invitational? Opened? Nourishing? It's unrealistic. Better to keep your guard up, play it safe, and be ready to back away if things get too disappointing. But that's not the way of Jesus. Is His way too risky? Is it really worth it?

Like Jesus

"Spiritual formation" has become such a comfortably common phrase in our Christian vocabulary that I wonder if we've lost sight of what it would actually mean to have Jesus formed in us. Do we really believe we're being spiritually formed if we experience the presence of Jesus without being empowered to relate like Jesus? Is effectiveness in ministry the best measure of maturity? Or is connection in community, a kind of connection that at least dimly reveals the relational life of the Trinity, a more reliable indicator that Christ is being formed in us?

Jesus told His followers that if they have seen Him, they've seen the Father. He came to reveal the relational beauty of God, a God who *moves* into our ugliness and need and *invites* us to enjoy His beauty and treasure. Look for a moment at how He related to others in ways that define relational femininity.

- "Come to me" (Matt. 11:28). Jesus issued an open invitation to people who He knew would not respond. How did it make Him feel?
- "How often I have wanted to gather your children together . . . but you wouldn't let me" (Matt. 23:37 NLT). Had Jesus drawn them by being more sensitive to their felt needs, no doubt He could have attracted more people more quickly. But He invited them to enjoy what they didn't realize they needed: an undeserved intimacy with God that

would release them to love others well no matter how little love was returned. Only a few were interested.

- "He . . . had no beauty that we should desire him" (Isa. 53:2). An appropriately disturbing title of a biography of Jesus might be *Beauty Displayed, Beauty Unseen: The Story of the Invisible God.*

No woman is naturally drawn to living the life of an invisible woman. No woman wants her biography to be titled *No Beauty to See: The Story of an Invisible Woman.* Every woman longs to be seen, to be taken into account, to not be dismissed, to be wanted and valued and enjoyed and respected. Invisibility is a woman's core terror—displaying what nobody sees, offering what nobody wants. Living in slavery to that fear requires that she not take the risk of relational femininity, that she relate in whatever fashion protects her unseen soul from feeling its loneliness. She then lives with a stubbornly closed heart and an angry refusal to nourish anyone with tenderness that might not be appreciated.

But that's not the way of Jesus. He never closed His heart. He never refused to offer life-giving love, even when doing so required Him to will His own death. Does a woman want *that* Christ formed in her? The woman drawn to God's call of relational femininity is the woman who believes that perfect love can release her from the enslaving power of fear. When a woman hears God's call to invite others to enjoy a beauty they may not see as a call to foolish risk-taking, she reveals that she is a woman who has not yet tasted what it means to be "perfected in love." That woman does not know what it means to be loved.

The Power of Fear

Let me unpack this idea of fear's power a little more. No woman living in slavery to fear, whether recognized or not, will be able to receive criticism or abandonment as an opportunity to discern if she has revealed Christ in the way she related. Only a woman freed from the control of fear will even ask the question. If a woman liberated by love humbly believes she is being criticized or rejected for relating like Jesus, she will count it a privilege to share in His sufferings and will pray that the one who has hurt her will see God's beauty. But if, when criticized or rejected, she is convicted to confess that fear took over, that she erected defenses around herself that hid Christ's beauty, she will gladly repent of sinfully falling short of God's relational glory and will long to be further perfected in His perfect love. She will ask her critic, the one who has moved away from her, for forgiveness. Either way, she will rest.

But notice what questions rise up in the rejected woman still enslaved by fear: *Do I have any value at all? What do I have that anyone could want?* She answers those terrifying questions by *doing*. She thinks, *I'll change the world. I'll lose weight. I'll be responsible to do everything right, to be there for everyone. I will find my value. I will be noticed and respected, never dismissed, maybe even wanted.* She becomes an *overwhelmed* woman, hiding her worthlessness behind overcommitment, making lists every morning of what she must do before sunset. She knows no rest and no joy, only pressure.

If the overwhelmed woman takes a long enough break from responsibility, she realizes she is really an *abandoned* woman. No one is there for her. She must take care of everyone. Her world will collapse if she fails anyone. She feels new waves of pressure moving through her soul. *I must manage everything. Married or single, widowed or divorced, in a small group or sitting alone in church, I am alone. No one sees me. No one wants to be with me, to do for me, to move into my heart.*

But why? The overwhelmed and abandoned woman spirals down into her buried center, and discovers that she is an *invisible* woman. Of course she has to *do* everything, because she *is* nothing. Of course she is abandoned. There is nothing in her that anyone would want. Confronted with this, she creates a substitute life in order to give the image that she exists and is worthy.

Fear has done its work. The devil chuckles with satisfaction. The vision of relational femininity is hidden behind dark clouds. The terror-driven woman sees no option but to declare:

- I will protect myself.
- I will retreat from pain.
- I will hide behind a socialized, perhaps even a Christian, persona.
- I will disappear into a fantasy world if I'm forced to give up any hope of keeping myself together in the real world.
- I will harden myself until the calluses covering my heart protect me from criticism, rejection, or abuse.
- I will live for whatever happiness or relief I can find.

Fear destroys femininity. The overwhelmed woman, managing life on her own as an abandoned woman, lives as a slave to her core terror of being an invisible woman, a woman with no beauty that anyone would desire.

The masks go on. Personas become fixed. Fig leaves cover shame. Terrible fear goes underground. And women survive. But no woman controlled by fear really lives. Survival takes many forms, yet none of them reveal the beauty of God.

11

WHAT FEAR CAN DO

Four Personas That Hide Women

Fearing people is a dangerous trap, but trusting the LORD means safety.

Proverbs 29:25 NLT

Thus says the LORD: Cursed is the man who trusts in man and makes flesh his strength, whose heart turns away from the LORD. He is like a shrub in the desert, and shall not see any good come. He shall dwell in the parched places of the wilderness, in an uninhabited salt land.

Jeremiah 17:5–6[1]

Every once in a while our Lord gives us a glimpse of what we would be like if it were not for him.

Oswald Chambers[2]

When the fear of what another person could do to her controls a woman, she is walking into a trap. When she trusts her own wisdom and depends on her own resources to avoid the trap and overcome her fear, she will live

---

1. In this passage, *man* means human being, male or female.
2. Oswald Chambers, *My Utmost for His Highest* (Uhrichsville, OH: Barbour, 1963), December 23.

"like a shrub in the desert," and bear no fruit that will bring anything good into her life or through her life. In a land uninhabited by relationships, in community with no connection (which is no community at all), a fear-controlled woman will thirst for soul-satisfying water that she cannot find.

She will "dwell in the parched places of the wilderness," living alone no matter who surrounds her. Her resources will be exposed as insufficient to create even the illusion of joy when disaster comes. For her, shattered dreams will mean a shattered life.

The woman controlled by fear will either die or merely survive. As long as fear rules her life, she will never know what it means to be fully alive as a feminine woman for the glory of God. She will realize in her heart that something is missing, that something is wrong. And when her resources fail, she will have her best opportunity to hear the good news of Jesus: that as a forgiven woman she can truly live.

In this chapter, I give four brief glimpses of how women survive without self-denying dependence on Christ, without life-anchoring knowledge of the Father, and without pride-weakening trust in God's Spirit to free them from slavery to the fear of invisibility:

Glimpse 1: The Defensively Deranged Woman

Glimpse 2: The Prematurely Satisfied Woman

Glimpse 3: The Angrily Hardened Woman

Glimpse 4: The Visibly Troubled Woman

No glimpse of a woman living in parched places is pretty. Perhaps you will see yourself in these glimpses. As you read, keep in mind that no woman, no matter how painful her life or powerful her fear, is beyond the reach of perfect love. The way *up* to living in the vision of relational femininity is preceded by the way *down* into the felt experience of paralyzing fear. Only from the bottom of the pit can we clearly see the top of the promise, that everyone is invited to come to Christ—and live!

Glimpse 1: The Defensively Deranged Woman

In the final minutes of a counseling session, my client, a middle-aged woman, suddenly stood up, tilted her head to look at the ceiling of my office and, with a little girl's smile of innocent joy, asked, "Is that you, Frank?" Then just as suddenly she sat down and looked at me. Still with a smile, though now one twisted into a knowing smugness, she announced, "Frank sings to me every night. It's wonderful. I feel so special." (I later learned she was referring to Frank Sinatra.)

When I was in training to become a psychologist, a wise, seasoned professor told me, "You will never understand human nature and why it goes awry until you understand how the anguish of unsatisfied desire ignites a fear that can make psychosis seem reasonable, a person's only hope for happiness." His words came back to me as I counseled with this woman.

Several sessions later, for reasons I did not understand then and do not clearly understand now, she lapsed into lucidity for more than five minutes. Perhaps somewhere in her image-bearing soul she sensed that I sincerely wanted to *know* her more than I wanted to professionally *treat* her. Perhaps in the safety of a tasted relationship that she had feared would never be hers to enjoy, she found the courage to let me meet the terrified woman hiding beneath her delusions. Speaking clearly and with genuine emotion, she told me what happened on her wedding night, thirty years earlier.

"When we got to our hotel room, my husband unpacked a few things then quickly turned on the television. He found the ball game I guess he was looking for and sat down to watch it. I felt like I wasn't even in the room. My father never saw me either, even when I cried. I needed my husband to see me, so I walked over to him, stroked his hair and whispered in his ear, 'I'll be back in a few minutes.'

"I disappeared into the bathroom and soon came out wearing a satin nightgown I was saving for this special night. He looked at me and said that I looked great. And then he went right back to watching the game. I wanted to scream, to say 'I'm here! Aren't I more attractive to you than a ball game?'

"But I said nothing. I took three sleeping pills, climbed into the king-sized bed and fell asleep. The next morning he was furious that I didn't wait up till the game was over to have sex. He told me he 'screwed' me while I was asleep. I hated that word. I hated what he did to me. I hated him. I still do. And I still hate that word."

Her wedding night was defined by an invitation with no response; worse, by an opening that was violently entered without permission. During the next thirty years, she seduced a dozen men. For the past several years, she had been listening to Sinatra's music for hours every day as she slowly slid into full-blown psychosis.

It's certainly possible that faulty brain chemistry predisposed her to retreat into a world of her own making. But I think my old professor had a point. The anguish of unsatisfied desire plunged her deeply into her core terror, the devastation of inviting someone who never came. In the time of trauma, her "normal" resources failed. She numbed her fear through defensive derangement, finding only in fantasy the illusion of beauty within her that could attract another.

Glimpse 2: The Prematurely Satisfied Woman

If clinically diagnosable women are (thankfully) a small minority, prematurely satisfied women are a large majority. I think of them as the "Ladies of Laodicea," an informal society of women bound together by complacency: they find their contentment in life's blessings.

Among their number, you will find happily married women, mothers of well-behaved and healthy kids, gifted Bible teachers, sociable women known for their hospitality, attractive women who dress tastefully, successful professionals and business leaders, talented musicians and authors, and caring women who reach out to others in need.

If they feel burdened by responsibilities, they feel *nobly* overwhelmed. When an unfamiliar sense of abandonment or loneliness threatens to shatter their contentment, time with good friends or an evening with their attentive husband restores their complacent satisfaction in blessing, a satisfaction they mistake for joy. Suggest to the Ladies of Laodicea that a core terror energizes much of what they do, that their good deeds serve to suppress a deep fear, and the suggestion will likely be dismissed without thought.

I need to be clear. It is *right* to find enjoyment in blessings. "It is a good thing to receive wealth from God and the good health to enjoy it. To enjoy your work and accept your lot in life—this is indeed a gift from God" (Eccles. 5:19 NLT). But it is wrong, and dangerous, to depend on blessings in this world for sustaining joy. Paul told Timothy to "Teach those who are rich in this world not to be proud and not to trust in their money, which is so unreliable. Their trust should be in God" (1 Tim. 6:17 NLT). And

Peter tells us that if we "want to enjoy life" we must relate well, using our tongue to speak life into others (see 1 Pet. 3:10–12 NLT).

While the defensively deranged woman enjoys *the beauty of fantasy*, the prematurely satisfied woman smothers her core terror by identifying and embracing only those desires that blessings in this world can satisfy. The deeper longing to know God and to make Him known in the middle of both blessings and difficulties remains safely unfelt or only weakly felt. With Satan's help and encouragement from her flesh, she manages to feel together and alive as she enjoys *the beauty of blessings*, with no serious concern to reveal God by the way she relates.

A friend of mine reliably smiles and says, "Isn't God good!"—a statement, not a question. "Good" is her favorite word. She is happily married to a good man, has two really good kids, enjoys a good ministry as a Bible teacher in a good church, welcomes good friends into her home for a good time, and reports many unusually good moments every morning with Jesus.

I asked her once, "Would you say God is good if something bad happened?" She looked puzzled, then patronizing. "I don't believe a good God allows bad things to happen to His children. If He does, it's always for a good purpose. In His hands, whatever looks bad will soon become good."

This woman has an extreme case of a common malady: false optimism. She is prematurely satisfied, enjoying her blessings as her greatest treasure and naively (and wrongly) counting on God to keep them coming. Suffering has little place in her understanding of the Christian life. Whatever fear exists in her soul lies deeply buried beneath false optimism that she mistakes for trusting God. She relates to others with little spiritual power.

Glimpse 3: The Angrily Hardened Woman

When others fail her, a certain kind of woman may numb her pain and fear beneath an indignant spirit of entitlement. *I deserve better and I'm justified in doing whatever I must to arrange for the treatment from others to which I'm entitled.* This woman becomes hard, angrily determined to escape pain by controlling her life and everyone in her life that is important to her. She may become a demanding wife, a domineering mother, or a distancing friend.

The angrily hardened woman sees no need to retreat into a world of fantasy. She feels quite able to control the real world. She refuses to contentedly find satisfaction in whatever blessings come her way. Although she may appear to be a charming, helpful, sincere Christian woman, she is constantly maneuvering to bring things under her control. Without realizing it, she feels as entitled to good treatment from others as God is entitled to worship.

She finds beauty in neither fantasy nor blessings but in power. She survives on *the beauty of relational power*. To the degree that others yield to her authority, she feels no fear. The angrily hardened woman scorns the idea that she is a terrified women and that she is living to avoid what she fears would destroy her soul. But she lives alone in an uninhabited land.

An ex-wife has launched a campaign to turn everyone against her former husband, including her children. Those who argue that she has been badly mistreated become her close friends. She distances herself from the few who question whether her decision to divorce was biblically justified. She openly scorns those who remain supportive of her ex-husband. Many in her church community value her ministry activities and see her as an abused Christian woman who is pressing on for Christ. She refused to continue with the counselor she was seeing during the divorce proceedings when he encouraged her to explore a root of bitterness that became obvious to him. She is an angrily hardened woman who numbs loneliness with relational power over others that provides her the pleasure and safety of control.

Glimpse 4: The Visibly Troubled Woman

The self-aware woman is troubled. When others see how troubled she is, they may regard her as immature, in need of help to become a prematurely satisfied woman. But they are wrong. If her trouble comes from realistic self-awareness, she is more able to hear God than women who successfully deny their deep fears. Women who fit this fourth glimpse have the most hope of moving from isolated survival to relational success.

This woman doesn't run into fantasy to escape her fears. She enjoys her blessings but keenly feels the anguish of wanting what nothing in this world can provide. Because she knows that she is not the woman she was meant to be, her humbled soul never hardens.

For reasons that may not be clear to her, she resists hiding from reality through daydreams. She refuses to pretend that all is well. And she realizes that she has the least control over what matters most. Because she honestly faces both her life and her heart, she is opened to feel her deepest longings as a woman and to face her worst failures as a woman.

The troubled woman, humbled by reality, has eyes that can see the vision God has for her. The fear of never becoming who God created her to be may, for a season, blind her to a vision that if seen would feel more frustrating than hopeful. But her awareness of unsatisfied desire and relational failure keeps her searching for more. And she sees the gap between the vision of relational femininity that the Spirit presents and the reality of where she is on her journey through life.

In brokenness over both her failure and her helplessness to change, a prayer rises to God from the center of her soul: "God, I come to You. Do with me as You want. Embrace me in Your perfect love that casts out all fear."

The troubled woman doesn't see beauty in fantasy, blessings, power, or even in herself. As she honestly and passionately searches for what is missing in her life, she comes to see that the beauty she longs to enjoy is in Jesus and in the Father He reveals. The fear that she has no beauty another could desire fades into irrelevance. Her core terror loses its power in the presence of perfect love. Her soul is captured by the Spirit-revealed beauty of Jesus.

Over time she realizes that she no longer feels driven to escape her fear or compelled to find affirmation of her beauty. Preoccupation with herself is slowly displaced by worship of God.

In the hands of God's Spirit, the terror He exposes surprisingly becomes an avenue into God's presence. As she responds to Christ's invitation to come to Him, something wonderful happens. The chains of her slavery to fear fall off, and she becomes aware of a desire stronger than all others, a desire to reveal the beauty of her opened and nourishing invitational Lord to others. The troubled woman then resonates with these words from Scripture:

> God is love. When we take up permanent residence in a life of love, we live in God and God lives in us. This way, love has the run of the house, becomes at home and mature in us, so that we're free of worry on Judgment Day—our

standing in the world is identical with Christ's. There is no room in love for fear. Well-formed love banishes fear. (1 John 4:17–18 Message)

The beauty of Jesus becomes visible in the midst of ongoing trouble, precisely because she no longer is obsessed with whether she is beautiful. It is enough that Jesus is beautiful and that she lives in Him. The visibly troubled woman travels through fear and despair toward becoming a woman fully alive in her femininity for the glory of God. The road she travels is narrow. In Part IV, we will look more carefully at the nature of this journey.

For now, we need to explore the core terror in men.

12

THE CORE TERROR OF A MAN

Weightlessness

The world has reached a major watershed in its history, equal in importance to the turn from the Middle Ages to the Renaissance. It will demand from us a spiritual blaze; we shall have to rise to a new height of vision, to a new level of life.

Alexander Solzhenitsyn[1]

Doubts prove that we are in touch with reality, with the things that threaten faith as well as with things that nourish it. If we are not in touch with reality, then our faith is apt to be blind, fragile, and irrelevant.

Frederick Buechner[2]

Think about it. If a man is masculine only to the degree in which the way he relates reveals the incarnational beauty of the God who hears us, remembers us, looks into us, and moves toward us, then the great majority of men (including the many who are quite satisfied with their manliness or never give it a serious thought) are simply not masculine.

1. Jimmy Long, *Emerging Hope* (Downers Grove, IL: InterVarsity Press, 2004), 72.
2. Ibid., 177.

- How many men really tune in to the deep hurts and worries of their wives, children, aging parents, and friends? How many men *hear* others?

- How many men are so gratefully overwhelmed with remembering God's movement into their lives that they can think of nothing more meaningful than moving similarly into someone else's life? How many men *remember* God?

- How many men probe with gentle curiosity into the inner world of their wives or girlfriends, willing to discover struggles they have no idea how to solve, willing to face a woman's disappointment that exposes a man's failure? How many men *look* deeply into others?

- How many men hear and see a woman's struggles and, rather than immediately trying to solve them, stay with her in her pain, praying for the wisdom to move wisely into her life? How many men *move* toward women motivated by the pure love of Christ? How many men *relationally* move toward others with the confidence that God can do miracles through them if their goal is to reveal, not themselves as worthy of appreciation, but the God who can change people into "little Christs"?

Measure a man by those standards and he falls short. Why? And why do so few men even think about what it might mean to reveal God by living relationally masculine lives?

Failing in Fear

Few women live with relational femininity as their compelling vision. Women find it easier to remain protectively closed than invitationally open and too often see nothing wrong with how they relate. Why? Is it because the men in their lives are not moving toward them? Have fathers failed to respectfully explore and enjoy their daughters' feminine souls? More than any man can realize, it is difficult for a woman to remain open when no man shows interest in entering into who she is as a beautiful woman.

But the *failure* of femininity has more to do with a woman's *fear* of femininity, a fear that only perfect love (which no man but One can provide) renders powerless. No woman perfectly rests in perfect love, and no woman will until heaven. The core terror of invisibility is therefore operating in every woman's life, to some degree. Rejection feels like a death blow. Fear convinces women to dress in the fig leaves of external beauty, perhaps to wear masks of competence and achievement or to present a persona of cheerful togetherness that hides a lonely person. Many women keep secret their shame and fear. The result? Women fall short of God's call to reveal His invitational beauty by the way they relate.

What about men? What fear keeps a man from relating with God-revealing masculinity?

Men are *doers*. We don't naturally give patient attention to another's hurts. No man remembers and celebrates God's movement into his life so gratefully that his consuming and controlling passion is to imitate that movement by the way he relates to others in every relationship, in every moment. It's rare for a man to look with nondefensive and nonevaluative curiosity into the hidden world of another. It's common for a man to wonder why a struggling person won't just "shape up." The courage required of a man to stay warmly involved with someone whose problems he cannot fix is in short supply. Few men move with humble confidence that God has given them the weight they need to meaningfully impact another's soul, a confidence that frees them to inquire into the impact they have made on another.

By these standards, randomly pick any one man and, more than likely, you will discover he is not masculine. Why? Have the women in his life not affirmed his efforts to move? Does his wife criticize his faults more than affirm his virtues? Are father wounds the cause?

Or is it something else? To at least some degree, every man falls short of the call to reveal God's incarnational beauty by relating as masculine men.

- Men don't *hear* well.
- Men don't *remember* God as their greatest joy.
- Men don't *look* into others with patient curiosity.
- Men don't *move* wisely into the lives of those they claim to love.

Why? To put it simply, we're scared to death. Fear controls us, far more than we know. High blood pressure has been called the heart's silent killer because we feel no symptoms while the damage happens. Likewise, men feel free, strong, successful, and alive even while they remain enslaved to an unfelt terror. That terror is the soul's silent killer.

Men are reluctant to acknowledge the existence of fear within them, and if it is acknowledged, its depth and power are dismissed. They may agree that the unexamined life is not worth living, but like men whose fear of prostate cancer keeps them too busy to see a doctor, they rarely find time to look deeply into the motivating energy beneath their relational lives. Getting on with life seems more productive than getting *into* life, especially into relational life.

In the next chapter, I get into *my* life, searching for both the terror that lies buried in my soul and for the hope buried even deeper. Because men are all pretty much alike beneath the surface, you may see in yourself what I see in me. But for now, sit quietly for a moment with King David. Pray the words he recorded in his personal prayer journal.

> O LORD, you have examined my heart
>   and know everything about me. . . .
> Such knowledge is . . .
>   too great for me to understand!
> I could ask the darkness to hide me
>   and the light around me to become night—
> but even in darkness I cannot hide from you. . . .
> Search me, O God, and know my heart;
>   test me and know my anxious thoughts.
> Point out anything in me that offends you,
>   and lead me along the path of everlasting life. (Ps. 139:1, 6,
>   11–12, 23–24 NLT)

Weightless

Before I explore my core terror, I should point out that women and men share the same basic fear of human existence. Because we were wired to breathe the life-giving air of community, we cannot endure the thought of isolation. We fear *aloneness*—life without connection, achievement without companionship, existence without friendship, forever wandering in lonely despair.

Loneliness is a taste of hell. Women experience the basic fear of aloneness as the terror of invisibility: unseen and unwanted. The call to invite others to move toward them arouses their fear. The question burns quietly within them: *Do I have beauty that another would desire?*

Men, created and called to move into relationship with others, feel the fear of aloneness differently. In their aloneness, men fear weightlessness. *Do I have what it takes to move into community, into soul-to-soul connection? To risk that my moving will have no visible impact? To move toward others who might not value my movement?*

When I write about women, I write as an outsider. I can hope for no stronger response from women who read my words than, "Not exactly, but close." When I write about men, I write as an insider. I want to seize that advantage. If I tell my story, perhaps other men will recognize their own.

I long to live in the "spiritual blaze" of masculinity, to heed Solzhenitsyn's call to let this world see the spiritual blaze of relationship as God designed it. But compared to the blazing life of Jesus, my life is a flickering candle. Will I ever catch fire? Doubts threaten to extinguish the flame. But Buechner's words inspire the courage to embrace my doubts as a means of facing unpleasant reality. I fall short of the relational glory of Christ every day. My failure so easily becomes a darkness that hides the reality of hope.

But when I search through my doubt and face the fear that my failure to move like a man will leave me disconnected, something unexpected happens. I discover my center as a Christian man. I discover my desire to move toward others the way God moves toward me. And then I feel more acutely the fear of men and hear more clearly God's call to men. And the battle of a lifetime begins: the struggle between the flesh and the spirit, the struggle between my devil-inspired fear and my desire to release the God-given life within me.

What is the terror in men that gets in the way of relating like men? The core terror is difficult for men to identify, hard for men to see, and even harder for men to own as a real problem. The infamous male ego gets in the way.

Let me now take a risk. I want to honestly explore the fear in the man I know best. I draw my inspiration for so foolish a venture from C. S. Lewis. When readers of *The Screwtape Letters*, the story of how demons tempt humans, assumed that Lewis had learned the ways of hell "by many years' study in moral and ascetic theology," Lewis replied, "They forget that there is an equally reliable, though less creditable way of learning how temptation works. 'My heart'—I need no other's—'showeth me the wickedness of the ungodly.'"[3]

I need no life other than my own to learn about men's core terror. If I successfully uncover the fear in other men, it has mostly to do with a painful look in a mirror surrounded by the light of sixty-six love letters from God to me.

3. C. S. Lewis, *The Screwtape Letters* (New York: Macmillan, 1961), xiii.

13

RECOGNIZING THE TERROR IN A MAN

God gave us a spirit not of fear but of power and love and self-control.

2 Timothy 1:7

As I write this, I'm scheduled to speak at a college chapel service tomorrow. Anticipation is mixed with indifference and fear. Why do I not care as I want to? What am I afraid of?

After sixty-eight years of living, sixty as a Christian, forty-six as a husband, forty-four as a father, forty as a psychologist, thirty-six as an author and speaker, and all sixty-eight as a male, I'm disappointed. I thought by now I'd be more mature than I am. I felt more mature when I was forty.

I've earned a somewhat deserved reputation as an honest struggler, a doubting Thomas who longs to be a faithful Paul but who lives more like an erratic Peter, and who descends too easily into the gloom of a William Cowper. Some people find comfort for their troubled souls in my struggles. Others think I need to more prayerfully practice spiritual disciplines or take Prozac.

I resonate with the postmodern emphasis on authenticity in community, on transparency as a lost virtue in the church that needs to be recovered. No one heals in hiding. But I want more than warm acceptance when I show myself. I want to hear truth that has the power to transform me, to set me free from fear. I've come to realize, however, that truth merely taught has little power. God's truth becomes credible when it is visibly plausible, when publicly declared truth is personally embodied in how the truth-declarer *relates*. Otherwise truth comes across as just a bunch of words, dry orthodoxy that makes people more smug than holy.

I do believe, though, that truth revealed by God is revealed in words—the words of Scripture. It's simply there, and it's true whether I believe it or not and whether I feel it or not. It exists outside of me. But objective truth, what God reveals, is also relational truth revealed by a relational God. And He intends that we experience His truth subjectively, in a community of truth-seeking worshipers who together long to reveal God by the way we relate, to each other and in the world.

And there's the rub. I teach more truth than I experience, far more. The gap between what I believe and what I live raises doubts, perhaps in others about me and certainly in me about myself and what I believe. I know the gap is supposed to breed humble, dependent faith in my heart. Sometimes it does. But even then doubt remains, like a cloud covering the morning sun.

Acedia is the result. *Acedia*: the inability to care deeply about anything, apathy toward opportunities for both pleasure and ministry that once excited me, boredom that drains the spirit of adventure out of life. Acedia greets me nearly every morning. Dostoyevsky defined hell as the suffering of being unable to love. Perhaps I'm living in the outskirts of hell when I suffer the inability to care. Am I tasting hell? Am I living in its neighborhood? Is love an objective decision that one can willfully choose without passion? Can I care without *feeling* care? Should I just buck up and make myself do better?

Paul told Timothy to continue *living* the truth of what he had learned and now "firmly believed" (see 2 Tim. 3:14). I sometimes feel so exhausted that I can't remember what I've learned and have taught for so many years. Firm belief can seem like a distant dream.

Why do I feel so empty, so passionless? Am I afraid? Has some swamp of terror become the breeding ground for the devouring insects of futility? Does a strange fear that I have nothing to offer extinguish my desire to offer anything? I hear stories that one man can change the world. Over my desk hangs a plaque with D. L. Moody's famous words: "The world has yet to see what God can do in and through and for and by a man whose heart is totally His. I will do my utmost to be that man." Those words, at the moment, do not excite me as they once did.

Shouldn't God do more *in* me before He expects more *of* me? Shouldn't He make His presence more tangible, His story more visible? I think I'm angry at God. I shouldn't be, I know. In Jesus He's given me everything. But His everything doesn't always feel like everything.

Mayberry

A five-year-old boy still lives in this sixty-eight-year-old man. Then I lived in a Mayberry-like town outside of Philadelphia, a town where, like Opie, I could walk home from kindergarten without fear. It was only six blocks. And Deputy Fife was always on duty. Life was good. I was safe. I was not alone.

But one spring day, as I was sauntering home after school, a butterfly caught my attention. I followed its flight and ended up lost on an unfamiliar street, one I had never walked on before.

I panicked. I had no confidence that I could find my way home. Movement seemed terrifying. So I stood still and cried. Within minutes that felt like a lifetime, a patrol car pulled up. Sheriff Taylor was on his way to meet Helen Crump for afternoon coffee. He saw me, stopped, got out of his car, and asked, "Hey there. What's wrong, little buddy?"

"I'm lost."

"Where do you live?"

"With Mommy and Daddy."

Just as he was about to ask me something else, a green 1950 Ford came racing up the street: my father's car. I later learned that Mother had called Dad. "Honey, Larry should be home by now. I don't know where he is. I called the school and he left almost an hour ago. You've got to find him."

When I saw my father, I was no longer afraid. A little embarrassed maybe, but not afraid. I was going home. Lesson learned:

> I am not adequate to move into life. I wish I could make it without help, but I can't. Will someone always come when I need them? I hope so.

Fast-forward three years. I'm now at Sandy Hill Boys Camp in Maryland, an eight-year-old boy away from home for the first time. One night around a blazing campfire, a counselor spoke to the campers and said, "Boys, look at the fire. You have a choice to make. Accept Jesus as your Savior or burn in the fires of hell forever."

For the second time, I knew I needed help. A policeman was good. Dad was better. Jesus was best—and necessary. Lesson learned, a lesson reinforced by a dozen more years of Sunday school and youth group:

> I can trust Jesus to keep me out of hell. And part of His job in the package deal is to never let my life feel like hell. I believe the words of the old Sunday school chorus: Every day with Jesus is sweeter than the day before. Life is good: Mayberry now, heaven forever.

Fast-forward once more, this time through the sixty years from my conversion to Christ right up until now. An undergraduate psychology professor told me I had the makings of a good psychologist. I earned a PhD in clinical psychology, graduating first in my class. I had a beautiful wife and two smart, healthy, athletic sons who became the foundation for a good life. I had a booming private practice, recognition as a preacher, author, and seminar leader, and enough money to live more than comfortably. Lesson learned:

> I do have what it takes. I can make life work. I am a success. I AM A MAN! I'm at home in Mayberry as an adult, and on my way to an even better city. Thank you Lord!

But every garden has weeds. My Mayberry has a hospital, a jail, churches wracked with tension, drug rehab centers, and counseling offices. The lesson learned through blessings began to wobble on its crumbling foundation.

- I was shamed by stuttering when a pastor asked me to close the service in prayer. I had asked God to let me speak fluently. I was twenty-two.
- I was bewildered when my wife of twenty years said with tears, "I don't want to grow old with you. It's just too painful." I thought the crisis we hit after eight years of marriage had been resolved.
- I was devastated by heart-wrenching difficulties in both my sons' lives. *God, I worked hard to be a good dad. What else did You want me to do?*
- I was crushed when two clients committed suicide. *Do I know anything about counseling people with real problems?*
- I was discouraged when a publisher told me in the 1980s that recent sales figures had downgraded me to a B-level author. *Am I losing what I once had?*

- I was overwhelmed with grief when my only brother died in a plane crash, when my mother developed Alzheimer's, when I watched my father sink into loneliness, and when I was struck with two bouts of cancer. *Are more surgeries ahead? Perhaps inoperable cancer?*

What happened to Mayberry? I learned a new lesson.

Nothing is guaranteed but the opportunity to know God in the best and worst of times, and at any time the power to move into other people's lives the way He's moved into mine. God calls that *life*. I know He's right.

But—do I know Him? Do I trust Him? Do I even *like* Him? Does He even exist? The questions of doubt rise up, even after all these years. Familiar verses meant to assure me of His love and goodness feel more like taunts.

- "I will never leave you nor forsake you" (Heb. 13:5).
- "When you pass through the waters, I will be with you . . . when you walk through fire you shall not be burned" (Isa. 43:2).
- "Come to me . . . and I will give you rest" (Matt. 11:28).
- "I have loved you with an everlasting love" (Jer. 31:3).
- "All things work together for good" (Rom. 8:28).

Faith and Doubt

I feel so alone. But to whom else can I go? Somewhere within me is a reality that only doubt can touch, a faith that reveals itself when despair leaves no other option. I *do* believe God. I *do* trust Jesus. I *do* know the Holy Spirit lives in me. And I *do* realize that because of His goodness He is devoting His power to making me a man, a man like Jesus who can find my joy in revealing God to others by the way I relate: *hearing* the cry of others and not dwelling on mine; *remembering* that knowing God, whether in a hospital bed or on a golf course, is life; *looking* to see into the broken hearts of others, to see the story beneath their cries; and *moving* into others' lives with the weight of God Himself, the weight of the glory that God gave to the incarnate Jesus, who now gives it to me.

And it's then, when faith surfaces and I hear God's call, that I feel terror, the terror of weightlessness.

- Can I hear the deep cry of another's heart? Do I even want to?
- Do I remember how God remembers me? Does worship rise from within me when life is hard? Or do I complain?
- Will I keep looking into another's life with gentle but relentless curiosity to see what's really there? Or do I want to see only those problems that I can do something about, as a competent man, not as a relational man?
- Am I praying for wisdom to discern how I can move with the life-changing impact of spiritual weight into someone whose life I've seen? Or do I let the fear of weightlessness paralyze relational movement and reduce me to a non-relational doer, a fixer, a petty manager of life?

Acedia is with me as I write these words. Everything feels like a chore, even flossing my teeth and counting out my daily dose of vitamins. I will speak at chapel tomorrow morning. But right now it feels more like an obligation than an opportunity.

—

Life seems pointless. I feel weightless. And yet the deeper I sink into the mud of despair, the closer I seem to come to my center. I am alive. I am forgiven. I do care. Acedia does not have the final word. My core terror is not my core center. *I am a man.*

And I hear God's call to enjoy relational masculinity. I discover my desire to live fully alive for the glory of God. Lesson learned:

Recognizing the terror in a man opens the door to pursuing life as a man. God's plan: be nothing in God's presence (other than His beloved) so that He can do anything in you and through you that He wants to do. Then you will become the someone God created you to be. D. L. Moody's words throb with new life.

Recognized terror opens the door to relational masculinity. Hidden terror opens the door to the more comfortable but wasted life of counterfeit masculinity.

14

WHAT FEAR CAN DO

A Glimpse into Three Weightless Men

The New Testament speaks emphatically of the "newness" . . . of the Christian's life in Christ, as compared and contrasted with all that went before.

J. I. Packer[1]

I know nothing about the wonderful experience of freedom from conflict and complete deliverance from every evil tendency. I have never won an inch of the way to heaven without fighting for it. I have never lived a day but I have had sorrow over my imperfection. I sometimes get near to God but at that time I weep most for my faults and failings.

Charles Spurgeon[2]

When a man comes before God terrified that he has no power to accomplish anything of more than passing significance; when he gets in touch with the emptiness in his soul that no achievement, recognition, or pleasure can fill; when he realizes that he falls short every day of how God designed him to relate; and when he admits that he has no grounds for requiring anything

1. Alister McGrath, ed., *The J. I. Packer Collection* (Downers Grove, IL: InterVarsity Press, 1999), 238.
2. Derek Tidball, *The Message of Holiness* (Downers Grove, IL: InterVarsity Press, 2010), 22.

from God and understands that he can only beg for mercy, it is then that his ultimate choice becomes clear:

EITHER bury his fear, emptiness, failure, and brokenness beneath an angry resolve to continue providing for himself whatever manageable and pleasurable satisfaction is available, and settle into self-centeredness as a familiar and comfortable way of life;

OR confess that he is a scared, empty, failing, and broken man, and gratefully surrender himself to God as a forgiven sinner and now a committed follower of Jesus Christ who is willing, at any cost, to become whoever God wants him to be and to move toward others however God leads him to move in order to reveal the radical other-centeredness of Jesus by the way he relates, by living the new way of the Spirit.

Until a man is humbled by acknowledging the fear that drives him, by admitting to an emptiness he cannot resolve, by realizing that the way he relates impacts no one deeply, and by bowing low in brokenness over how far short he falls of God's relational design for men, he will spend his life doing much that amounts to little.

How do men who are not masculine relate? How do they miss the opportunity to connect on the bridge? Let's take a look at three kinds of men, men who hide their fear *from* themselves and end up living *for* themselves.

Glimpse 1: The Shallow Man
Glimpse 2: The Secularized Man
Glimpse 3: The Spiritually Addicted Man

They are each traveling on the broad road that feels good for a while but leads them toward misery.

Glimpse 1: The Shallow Man

Shallow spirituality has always been popular. It's easy. As one concerned observer put it, God's glory, His weight, sits lightly on the American church, and on today's church perhaps more lightly than in earlier days.

Indifference to everything but personal comfort is one form of shallow spirituality that has long been with us, and continues to attract scores of

Christians today. For centuries, followers of Jesus have been trusting God for heaven later and have been naively trusting Him for the good life now, the good life of good health, good families, and good income—for every self-satisfying dream to come true. Spiritual Christians, it has been falsely assumed, are in line to receive everything they want in this world.

More recently, at least in evangelical circles, a new understanding of spirituality has won a following. Spiritual formation, not earthly blessings, is now recognized as the proper mark of a serious Christian. But in some circles the term's rich heritage has been weakened. In current thinking, spiritual formation has come to mean little more than *feeling close to God* and *a desire to change the world*. (Living a moral, decent, and generous life is an assumed part of the picture as well.)

Relating well to each other in Christian community as feminine women and masculine men is set aside as a more specialized concern, a side topic that makes for interesting discussion in limited groups, a way of living that is both controversial and inessential to true spiritual formation.

In the mystical quietness of spiritual retreats complete with *lectio divina* and contemplative prayer, and in the excitement of world-changing activism through political campaigns and working for social justice, something is often missing, something important. A passionate focus on *personal* spirituality, feeling God's presence, and *social* spirituality, changing the world through evangelism and social action, too often leaves little room for serious interest in *relational* spirituality.

Hours before Calvary, Jesus prayed that His followers would relate well, revealing to the world what divine community looks like (see John 17:20–26). Days after Calvary, He told us to "make disciples of all nations, baptizing them in the name of the Father and of the Son and of the Holy Spirit" (Matt. 28:19). Our power to make the difference in our world that God is interested in depends on how His world-changing disciples get along with each other. The order matters: relate well in order to serve well.

In His high priestly prayer before His crucifixion, Jesus, referring to us, said, "I pray that they will all be one, *just as you and I are one*. . . . May they experience such *perfect unity* that the world will know that you sent me and that you love them as much as you love me" (John 17:21, 23 NLT, emphasis added). It is only God-encountering grateful worshipers who, as Spirit-empowered God-revealers, relate like Jesus, as feminine women who are openly inviting and masculine men who lovingly move.

Let me put personal, social, and relational spirituality together in two sentences:

When a man's experience of God does not change the way he relates to others, his experience of God is either shallow or spurious. When a man's efforts to serve God in missional work, either through evangelism or social action, is not the overflow of Christ-revealing masculinity, his zeal will lack the power needed to reach deeply into people's hearts.

Here is my point: a shallow, non-relationally focused understanding of spirituality will produce shallow, non-relationally focused men. Experiencing God is a consuming privilege. Serving God is nonnegotiable. But knowing God in a way that forms us into relationally masculine men is critical.

Lyle illustrates my concern. Lyle serves God. He disciples men. He cooks food for homeless men in an inner-city soup kitchen. He spends one day a month in spiritual retreat and an hour every morning in personal devotions.

I know Lyle's wife. She approached me for counseling. "I feel invisible to my husband," she said. "When I hurt, he hugs me. He never asks why I'm hurting. When I get frustrated, he takes my hand and prays for me, then walks away with a satisfied smile. I feel like a little girl whose busy daddy takes time to pat her on the head. Lyle doesn't know me any better now than when we got married." Then she cried, "Is there nothing in me that Lyle wants to know?"

Her husband lives for personal power, to make an impact by what he does that identifies himself as a godly man. Lyle evangelizes the lost and disciples the found—and relates deeply with no one. He emerges from his morning devotions and monthly retreats more energized to exhibit his spirituality to others.

Spiritually shallow men "act religious, but they will reject the power that could make them godly" (2 Tim. 3:5 NLT). Why? They live separate from Christ. How? They hide their fear of weightlessness out of the reach of perfect love, beneath personal power that gains recognition but lacks depth. These men appear godly to many, but they know little of the Spirit's power that is available to change them before they go about changing the world, the power to spiritually form them into relationally masculine men who reveal God because they know God.

Lyle is a spiritually shallow man. He could be different.

Glimpse 2: The Secularized Man

Secularized men are cousins to shallow men. Both kinds of men do lots of things for God with little of God's power. The difference is this: shallow spiritual men do their obviously Christian work in Christian community. Secularized men serve Jesus in the marketplace as ethical Christians, as hardworking men of integrity in their businesses or professions who generously support and are sometimes actively involved in Christian ministries. Both wrongly define what it means to be a spiritually forming man.

Christianity turns our natural values upside down, especially our motivational and relational values. Nothing is secular in God's world. Everything centers on His kingdom purposes, so everything is either sacred or profane, never merely secular. Whatever we do, we're to "do it all for the glory of God" (1 Cor. 10:31 NLT). That upsets our naturally self-centered world. We're bent to live for our glory, for whatever provides us with the desired experience of personal weight.

But we've been given "everything we need for living a godly life" (2 Pet. 1:3 NLT). A godly life, above all else, is relational life, life in community. God is Himself a community of three Persons. The life of God in the soul of a man (to borrow the title of Henry Scougal's classic book) is *relational* life, and it evidences itself most clearly not through the ethics we follow, but through the kind of love we offer. And that kind of love, when received from God and released toward others, radically changes the way we relate.

Sometimes the excitement about God that men feel during a men's conference translates into a passion for Christian ethics displayed in the marketplace and for Christian ministries launched with marketplace resources. Both are good, but not if things stop there. If things go no further, spirituality is then secularized into a kind of ethical and ministry lifestyle that decent non-Christian men can adopt as easily as Christian men.

Jesus did not endure Calvary to help us live merely ethical lives but to transform the way we relate, from men who are curved in on themselves to men who curve outward into God-revealing, radically masculine lovers of God and others.

It is good when a Christian businessman is known for his fairness and integrity. It is better when he looks for and seizes opportunities to *hear* a colleague's loneliness, to *remember* the God who wants to bring that man to His party, to *look* closely enough to see that man's struggles and suffering and sin, and to *move* into that man's life with gospel truth delivered in gospel power with gospel wisdom and love.

The many virtues evident in a secularized man's life foster the illusion that he can think of himself as a good man while he relates badly, most often completely unaware that he is relating badly. For such a man, relational masculinity that reveals a relational God is rarely even a category to consider. Relational problems, therefore, with wives, girlfriends, children, or friends, are understood as evidence of another's failure.

One secularized man seemed nobly bewildered when he told me, "I don't get it. My wife is always on my back about something. Sometimes she's so critical I just explode. The only way I can keep loving her is to distance myself from her. For the life of me, I can't see what's wrong with her. I just want to get along, go to church together, do ministry together, and enjoy life together. I really hope you can help her."

A man who won't face his relational fear will never see his relational sin. A little pornography now and then, a lot of long workweeks, or even adultery or divorce will seem warranted. That man will not realize that the way he relates is stubbornly designed to protect him from his relational weightlessness, his inability to do anything of real value. He will continue to depend—for his all-important sense of personal well-being—on his *personal power*, his displayed power to do good things well.

Until the secularized man falls to his knees, broken over how badly he fails his wife and everyone else, pleading mercy for his relational sin and asking his wife to forgive him for the damage he's done to her soul, he will continue doing good things that a secular man could do and puzzling over why neither his wife nor his spiritual friends enjoy him as so many others do.

That man is not masculine. But he could be.

Glimpse 3: The Spiritually Addicted Man

I don't easily plead guilty to the sins of either the shallow man or the secularized man. I've never felt satisfied with personal power that fails to impact others deeply and does not move into the chaos and suffering of the human experience.

But a glimpse of a *spiritually addicted man* bears an uncomfortable similarity to whom I see when I look in a mirror.

A good friend tells me he is addicted to insight—biblical insight. From the pulpit or in conversation, he displays wisdom with the self-effacing but confident flair of a man who expects to be admired.

Another friend once annoyed me with a meddling question. He asked whether I thought I could spiritually impact others if my brainpower were diminished. I offered him three responses. One, I believe that presence, being with another with no agenda other than to connect as souls, has power to draw someone closer to the Lord. Two, I believe presence plus wisdom received in the mind and delivered through words has more power. Jesus came to be with us *and* to teach us. Three, I worry that I depend more on sharing wisdom than offering presence for the impact I want to make. I'm better at giving my mind than giving myself. It's less risky. Reject my wisdom and I can feel superior. Reject my soul and it hurts.

Many years ago when I was first becoming visible in the Christian world and recognized as a good thinker, I suffered a concussion. While I was stretched out on a hospital bed in the emergency room waiting for the results of an X-ray of my brain, I screamed for half an hour, "I'll never think again!"

I was terrified my god was dying.

I've listened to many pastors preach. One comes to mind who always shares something from the biblical text I've never seen before. My awareness of *me* makes me wonder about him. Which of two responses to his preaching would he value more? Would it be, "Pastor, the Lord spoke to me in deeply significant ways through your message today"? Or would it be, "Pastor, I'm amazed at what you can see in the Bible that I would never see without your help—you have such remarkable insight into God's Word"?

For a spiritually addicted man, affirmed wisdom means more than an influenced life. I wonder: Will you, my readers, be stirred by God's Spirit to become more relationally feminine or masculine? I pray so. Will you tell your friends that this is a must-read book and perhaps buy a dozen copies to give away? I hope so. Will the second response encourage me more than the first?

Spiritually addicted men let first things slide into second place. And second things, such as recognition for exhibited wisdom, happily climb into first-thing status.

Let me highlight our main points:

- Shallow men are satisfied with power without depth, rarely even noticing the lack.
- Secularized men enjoy the power to do good things, giving little thought to relating well according to God's definition.
- Spiritually addicted men display power over people through whatever resources they have that win respect and admiration.

Unless these men register concern that they may have a serious problem and plead with God's Spirit to search their hearts, they may never recognize their fear-driven, flesh-nourishing, self-sustaining way of relating—and never see it as bad. Without the Spirit's revealing work, none of these men will discover the desire and the power to reveal God to others by living as relationally masculine men. It could be so different.

And it will be, for the sincerely struggling man. The hopeful glimpse of that man deserves a separate chapter.

15

A FOURTH MAN

Males Who Are Becoming Masculine

When a man turns to Christ and seems to be getting on pretty well (in the sense that some of his bad habits are now corrected), he often feels that it would now be natural if things went along fairly smoothly. When troubles come along—illness, money troubles, new kinds of temptations—he is disappointed. These things, he feels, might have been necessary to rouse him and make him repent in his bad old days; but why now? Because God is forcing him on, or up, to a higher level: putting him into situations where he will have to be very much braver, or more patient, or more loving, than he ever dreamed of being before. It seems to us all unnecessary: but that is because we have not yet had the slightest notion of the tremendous thing he means to make of us.

C. S. Lewis[1]

Listen to the apostle Paul, who without question was a deeply spiritual man surrendered to the Spirit's work within him, describe what was going on in his inner world.

> "For I do not understand my own actions. For I do not do what I want, but I do the very thing I hate" (Rom. 7:15). I wonder what that thing was.

1. C. S. Lewis, *Mere Christianity* (London: Collins Fontana, 1955), 170.

"For I have the desire to do what is right, but not the ability to carry it out" (v. 18). Is this the same Paul who in other places gloried in the new covenant truth of a new heart that was empowered to do right?

"For I do not do the good I want, but the evil I do not want is what I keep on doing" (v. 19). Really, Paul? There were good things you had opportunity to do that you turned away from? And you actually did evil things you sincerely struggled not to do?

You may be aware of the debate generated by Paul's words in Romans 7. Was he talking about his life before he was born again, perhaps while he was coming under conviction of sin? Or was he describing his journey as a Christian, not as a novice but as a seasoned, tested, and spiritually forming believer? "Wretched man that I am! Who will deliver me from this body of death?" (Rom. 7:24). Are these the words of a Christian or a non-Christian?

No shallow man would be likely to utter those words. Neither would a secularized man. I can conceive of a spiritually addicted man hating the addiction he loves and saying something similar. But Paul's words are words that flow most painfully and desperately from the mouth of a sincerely struggling man.

Glimpse 4: The Sincerely Struggling Man

Both the exegesis of trusted scholars and the reality of my own experience throughout six decades as a Christian man persuade me that committed followers of Jesus will, if they are honest, repeat the words of Paul until they meet Jesus face-to-face.

Augustine's *Confessions*, the record of a struggling life, is a landmark classic. Spurgeon's words that opened chapter 14—"I have never lived a day but I have had sorrow over my imperfection"—give me hope. Great Christian men like Augustine and Spurgeon, and even Paul, struggled and sometimes failed. They did things they had no business doing. Like me!

But they understood that repentance opens the door to more consistently and fully living their new life in Christ, the new way of the Spirit. And they celebrated the truth that ongoing repentance, including daily repentance of relational sin, keeps the door open to the new way that God intends Christian men to live.

Paul, a man taught by Jesus Himself, a man whom God trusted to write so much of the New Testament, a man who actually glimpsed the unseen world before he died, could not always find the power to do the good he longed to do, but kept on, repeatedly, doing what he could only describe as evil. Can we expect to do better? Perhaps we should learn to praise God more for His grace than for our holiness.

Our way of thinking about spiritual victory might need revision, especially the triumphalist view that promises a kind of victory neither Augustine, Spurgeon, or Paul ever experienced. Here is one suggestion. The sincerely struggling Christian man (and certainly woman too) who lives in victory:

- will not live sinlessly but will on occasion fail badly in what he does and will often fail badly in how he relates
- will hate everything sinful even while he is powerfully drawn to its pleasures
- will struggle mightily against sin, always longing to know the power to live a holy life

The evidence of victory will consist of:

- brokenness over sin committed, whether sexual (such as adultery), behavioral (such as dishonesty), or relational (such as responding to offense with revenge)
- increasingly strong but fluctuating resistance to temptation, even as temptations weaken or grow in strength
- release of the power to love others even when defeated and broken, power that comes from a yearning and hopeful heart that celebrates not spiritual achievement but rather the grace of God that makes it possible

Listen again to Paul.

Something has gone wrong deep within me and gets the better of me every time.

It happens so regularly that it's predictable. The moment I decide to do good, sin is there to trip me up. I truly delight in God's commands, but it's pretty obvious that not all of me joins in that delight. Parts of me covertly rebel, and just when I least expect it, they take charge.

I've tried everything and nothing helps. I'm at the end of my rope. Is there no one who can do anything for me? Isn't that the real question? (Rom. 7:21–24 Message)

It is the real question, though not the question asked by either shallow or secularized men, and not the question asked passionately enough by spiritually addicted men. But it is the question that bursts from the heart of a sincerely struggling man.

And it is a question with an answer. That truth makes me want to shout, "All Glory to God!" And yet I must keep in mind that the question will need to be asked time and time again. I've been a sincerely struggling Christian for six decades and I've never stopped asking that question.

I know Christian men who have been involved in nearly every form of sexual sin, and some who still are. Strip clubs, sexual abuse, homosexuality, adultery, emotional affairs, cross-dressing, pornography, selfish sex with a spouse, prostitution, voyeurism, checking out attractive women at the mall—the list is long.

Are these men really Christians? Many are. Do they sincerely desire to follow Christ? Many do. Are they excusing their sin as something for which they bear little or no responsibility? Most aren't. Do they believe that forces beyond their control sometimes make it impossible to resist sinning? Not many. But to some degree, each of these men is sincerely struggling.

And they have an unasked-for advantage in their journey toward relational masculinity: *they cannot believe they are without sin.* The others, the shallow and secularized and spiritually addicted men, find it easier to live with little felt need to repent.

Walking by the Spirit

Paul told us to "walk by the Spirit" (see Gal. 5:16). But what does that mean? Whatever more it may mean, to walk by the Spirit includes being sensitive to and humbled by our daily failure to reveal God by the way we relate, calling relational sin evil and hating it, and praying fervently for the power to relate well as feminine women and masculine men who live for the central purpose of glorifying God by delighting in Him and revealing Him to others.

The more we walk by the Spirit, the more we will thrill to and live in the truths of Romans 8. We are:

- under no condemnation for sin
- controlled by the indwelling Spirit
- free to resist the world and the flesh and the devil
- no longer slaves to fear but alive to God
- warmly aware that our former Judge is now our Abba
- still groaning over temptations, over a messed-up world, and over unsatisfied desire, but waiting eagerly for the eternal day when struggle and sin will cease

Devoid of self-righteousness and free from the illusion of "having arrived," sincerely struggling men of God will feel their fear and face their sin with growing appreciation for the grace of God that frees them to love better, to relate as masculine men who hear the cry of others, who remember the love of God, who look into suffering and sinful souls, and who move with spiritual weight that can change lives, like Jesus.

PART III

IDENTIFYING OUR RELATIONAL SIN

The Opportunity for Life-Releasing Brokenness

What is causing the quarrels and fights among you? Don't they come from the evil desires at war within you? . . . If we claim we have no sin, we are only fooling ourselves.

James 4:1; 1 John 1:8 NLT

As men and women, we are designed and called to build God-like community by releasing into others what is most alive in us as new creatures in Christ. That community will develop to the degree that our overriding purpose as we relate to others is to please and reveal God, and to thus bring His heavenly kingdom of relational beauty to earth.

Yet when we are controlled by fear, we relate in order to protect ourselves from pain and to advance our experience of personal well-being.

Self-centered relating—relational sin—destroys community. When we live to relieve our gender-specific fears, we fail to reveal the beauty of God's relational nature. We then fail to honor the purpose for which we were created as male and female, to reveal how God relates within His divine community by relating with masculine or feminine expressions of Trinitarian love and to thus bring heaven's beauty into human community.

In this section of the book, we will explore two questions: How do unfeminine women relate? How do unmasculine men relate?

16

RELATIONAL SIN

Our Tongue—The Restless Assassin

Death and life are in the power of the tongue.

Proverbs 18:21

Let every person be quick to hear, slow to speak.

James 1:19

If anyone thinks he is religious and does not bridle his tongue but deceives his heart, this person's religion is worthless.

James 1:26

Look at the ships also: though they are so large and are driven by strong winds, they are guided by a very small rudder wherever the will of the pilot directs. So also the tongue is a small member, yet it boasts of great things.

James 3:4–5

How great a forest is set ablaze by such a small fire! And the tongue is a fire, a world of unrighteousness. . . . No human being can tame the tongue. It is a restless evil, full of deadly poison.

James 3:5–6, 8

Reflect with me as I consider what the Bible says about the tongue. Keep these thoughts in mind as we plow ahead and discuss the life-releasing opportunity of brokenness over relational sin and the easily overlooked and often minimized sin of a flesh-driven tongue.

- Relational sin is not incidental; it is deadly. Souls are destroyed by words, not bullets. No sword of steel is sharper or plunges deeper than the sword of the tongue.

- A ship is driven off course by strong winds, but a small rudder under the pilot's control can keep the ship heading toward the destination chosen by the pilot. If the pilot is foolish, the ship will move steadily toward shipwreck. If the pilot is wise, the ship will reach safe harbor. So, too, the tongue, no matter how strong the winds of rejection, neglect, fear, or failure, will steer the soul in one of two directions. Under the control of the flesh, the soul will shipwreck on the rocks of a commitment to preserving self. With the Spirit in control, the tongue will guide the soul to the safe harbor of revealing God, no matter how windy the trip.

- When words reflect the relational energy of the Trinity, it's unmistakable: supernatural power and Holy Spirit wisdom are in play. When words are used to protect and preserve one's self, it's irrefutable: natural power and fleshly foolishness have taken control.

- No sin is less recognizable in the moment of its commission or, because it seems so justified, more resistant to repentance than relational sin. And no violation of God-revealing femininity or masculinity is more dangerous to both the violator and the violated than words full of deadly poison.

- A woman is *least* feminine, not (as culture might suggest) when her hair is a mess or her figure is no longer svelte, nor when she is unseen and unwanted by others, but when her soul is closed and her words lock the door.

- A man is *least* masculine, not (as culture might suggest) when he makes little money or his body is weak, nor when he receives little recognition because he makes little impact, but when his soul is frozen and his words do more to protect him from feeling the pain of his assumed insignificance than to pour hope into others who feel empty and alone.

Each of us sins with our words every day. When the intent of our words falls short of revealing to others the relational glory of our inviting and moving God, we are sinful, and all the more so when we feel justified in using words either to protect ourselves from relational hurt or to advance our sense of well-being at some cost to another. We have new reason every day to thank Jesus for dying the death we deserve.

The more clearly we understand what it means to be relationally feminine or masculine, the more painfully we will recognize our relational sin. And that's good. Brokenness over falling short leads to repentance that embraces a compelling vision of becoming fully alive as women and men for the glory of God. The deeper the repentance, the richer the release of a passion to reveal God by the way we relate and through the words we speak.

Let me now pursue the purpose of Part III, to zero in on what gender-discordant relational sin looks like in everyday life and recognize how we violate our call to be feminine or masculine by the words we speak.

Relational Sin in Women

When a woman's words flow from her feminine soul, when they are spoken with the desire to reveal the invitational kindness of God, her listeners feel strangely drawn. No woman need feel pressure to carefully choose the right words that measure up to some standard. Words that invite come from a released desire to welcome and nourish godly movement in another.

Feminine words from one woman draw another woman into noncompetitive rest that overcomes the second woman's need to display or protect herself. And a woman's feminine words arouse a man, not to use her for his own pleasure, but to move toward her as a woman of value and worth. He *sees* her and wants to *know* her.

But unfeminine words, words that are energized by a demand to be seen and known, create either relational distance or counterfeit intimacy. When one woman relates to another woman in the energy of control or defense, their two souls never connect. Competition, jealousy, snubs, and threats create distance. Some kindhearted woman might respond to the pull of a needy female friend and provide affirmation that creates the illusion of closeness, but in fact she only deepens a fragile dependency.

Men respond to unfeminine words with irritable stiffness ("Will you stop trying to control me?"), stubborn retreat ("I don't want to talk about it!"), defensive challenge ("You might want to try accepting me once in a while."), or selfish exploitation ("C'mon, let's go to bed.").

It comes down to this: a woman's words will draw others to her or distance others from her. She will speak *either* with the feminine power of an openness that invites the best from another and embraces it when it comes *or* with unfeminine power designed to protect herself from another through control that drives people from her.

And that pattern will exhibit itself whether a woman is speaking as a wife, fiancée, date, sister, daughter, mother, friend, employer, employee, colleague, businesswoman, professional, pastor, small group member, director of women's ministries, counselor, or spiritual director. If you can think of any other platform from which a woman speaks, add it to the list.

Let me single out motherhood for illustration. Two women, Judy and Dianne, are both in their late fifties and are both understandably very concerned over sons who are in their late twenties. Each son is struggling, one in his marriage and with doubts about his faith, the other with drugs and angry disillusionment with Christianity.

Judy's Story

Judy, a committed Christian whose son is plagued by marital tension and spiritual doubts, worries that her otherwise good husband is not stepping up as he should by moving more directly into their son's life. Her concern may be warranted. Judy's urge to "help" is fueled by her struggling son and her passive husband. She feels the need to speak words to her son that her husband should be speaking.

Frequent phone messages and regular emails both express her motherly curiosity about how her son is doing and remind him of her standing offer to help in any way she can. Her calls and notes are rarely returned. However, eventually a luncheon conversation was reluctantly agreed to by her son. According to Judy's report, it went something like this:

"So, how are things with Marie?"

"About the same."

"Are you asking her how she's feeling? Women like to be explored by their husbands, you know."

"Some."

"Well, what does she say? Does she open up with you?"

"Mom, we'll work it out, okay?"

"Honey, I'm just trying to help. And I really think that the closer you get to the Lord, the better your marriage will be. Are you going to church? Maybe you could talk to the pastor. I know him. He's a good man."

"Mother, leave it alone."

"Okay, I understand. I respect your desire to deal with this on your own. I'm just saying that there are times when we all need a little help. And I'm praying that you'll think about what the Lord can do to help you grow and love your wife well. Prayer does make a difference, you know."

"You've made your point. Look, either we talk about something else or I'm going to leave."

Two days later, after reporting that conversation to me, Judy asked, "What more can I do? I really want to help. How can I get my husband to talk to him? I think he really needs his father's attention. I love my son so much."

This genuinely Christian woman had no idea that she was relating with her son and husband, and with me, in gender-discordant relational sin. Her son avoided her. Her husband endured her. And nothing in me was drawn to feminine beauty in her. Her words may sound merely a bit pushy to us, not really all that bad, but relational sin is like that. It often comes across as little more than inappropriate. However, in her son's ears, Judy's words convey a painful message: *You don't have what it takes to relate well. You have no weight. Let me guide you as I had to when you were a child.*

With the best of intentions, Judy was speaking words that were poisoning her son.

Dianne's Story

Dianne, mother of a rebellious, drug-abusing, church-hating son, handled things differently. In a letter to her son, she wrote:

> I long to see you living in a way that brings you joy. I am so grateful that you're my son. I love you as you are and will love you till the day I die. My heart breaks with sadness over how difficult your life has become and how badly the church has failed you. I pray that you will see Jesus extending to you the love and grace that His church failed to give. I am at peace as I write these words, and I will be forever grateful that I've been given the privilege of being your mother.

In this letter, I hear words of invitation, not demand. Rather than "helping" her son, Dianne opened her heart to him. After reading her letter,

I asked her, "You said you are at peace. And yet you've been praying for almost a decade that God would reach your son and, at least visibly, things have gotten worse. Why do you still pray? And what keeps you at peace as you continue to pray with no answers?"

With no trace of either self-pity or pride, Dianne answered, "I would not want to meet my Lord knowing I refused to talk with Him about a deep burden in my soul. I think it brings Him great pleasure when I open my heart to Him and trust Him to do whatever He knows is best. I want much else, but I want nothing more."

Dianne neither demanded change in another for her sake nor depended on change in another, change that she legitimately and deeply desired, for her continued faithfulness to God. She has since died and her son at last report is still far from God. But his mother is now at perfect peace. While Dianne lived, she displayed the beauty of relational femininity with her words, never perfectly and not always, but richly and often, even in the midst of profound heartache.

It is possible to reveal God in any circumstance, but a woman must know the battle she is fighting. The enemy is never a passive or abusive husband, or a rebellious son, or a critical parent or friend. Nor is it poor health, or no money, or panic attacks, or depression. A woman's enemy is her terror-driven urge to control her world, to relate with no higher priority than to protect her heart from hurt. That enemy can only be defeated by a Spirit-granted desire to reveal God's invitational nature through words that draw others to her with confidence, should they respond, that they will be nourished to become who they could be.

It is difficult for a woman, even a committed Christian woman, to realize that her efforts to change another are stained by a stubborn concern for her own well-being, a concern that compromises love. The invitational nature of Jesus is not revealed in the words of a woman whose peace depends on the response of another.

Relational Sin in Men

When a man's words speak life, others will recognize an opportunity to connect that either draws or frightens them. Men who are drawn will seize

the chance for two men to meet as they are, with little pretense or postur-
ing, and with a vision for mutual encouragement that will strengthen both
men to become whom they most want to be. Men who are frightened will
back away, often with dismissive scorn or anger.

Women who are drawn will, with caution, claim the opportunity to
open themselves as friend or lover with the grateful hope of being seen and
wanted and, even more, with the anticipation of receiving and nourishing
godly movement. Unfeminine women still controlled by fear will retreat
with caution to a self-protective, safe distance.

The opportunity for men and women to meet on the Bridge of Connection should be routinely available in Christian community. It is not.
Too often, men speak unmasculine words. They remain on their side of
the bridge, unwilling to risk failure should they try to relationally connect
by hearing, remembering, looking, and moving. Better to remain within
their sphere of competence where inadequacy is less likely to be exposed.

Relational sin in men, evidenced in words designed to display adequacy,
win respect, or create feelings of significance, never pours life into another.
Relational sin sucks life out of others. Wives feel untouched, children un-
explored, and friends unattached. Whether a man is speaking as a husband,
fiancé, date, brother, son, father, friend, employer, employee, colleague,
businessman, professional, pastor, small group member, director of men's
ministries, counselor, or spiritual director, his words will either stir life in
others or deaden the souls of others.

Two different men, each with the opportunity to connect as husbands,
come to mind. One man illustrates relational sin, the other relational holiness.

Nathan's Story

Nathan's wife descended into deep depression, suddenly and without
apparent cause. He, a pastor, resolved to be there for her, to walk with her
as she struggled with loss of desire to do much of anything.

His words to her sounded good to himself and to the few men at church
in whom he confided. "Honey, you'll get through this. God has not abandoned you. And I won't either. I'll always be here," he said. "When you feel
up to it, I'd like to take you away for a weekend, just to relax and recharge.
I don't care what it costs. I'll find a way to pay for it." His wife responded
with a weak smile that encouraged him.

Antidepressant medication slowly took the edge off her despair and brightened her black mood into dark gray. Nathan asked the psychiatrist what he could do to further help in her recovery. Sensing the possibility of impatience, the doctor cautioned that clinical depression could sometimes drag on for a long time. Nathan responded with a grave nod but thought to himself, *The doctor isn't a Christian. I believe in the power of prayer.*

Nathan continued to do all he could, and he felt good about his efforts. But they went unrewarded. Then something surprised him. The longer his wife's depression remained unchanged, the more he felt unable to resist sexual fantasies. For the first time he found himself searching the internet for porn sites that aroused him.

We met to talk.

"I don't know what's happening," Nathan said. "I really don't think these new sexual urges are entirely caused by my wife's lack of sexual interest. Our sex life has never been all that good. She's generally been cooperative but never eager. I suppose there has to be some connection between her depression and my sexual temptations. But I don't know what it could be. I think I've really been there for her, but maybe I'm not doing enough. She isn't getting better."

"What goes on inside you as you keep trying to help with no results?" I asked.

"Do you think I'm angry? I know I'm disappointed and pretty frustrated."

"Where have you failed before?" I continued. "Your church is growing, your kids are all doing pretty well, you did well in seminary."

"But I'm not failing. Every day I do whatever I can think of to make her life a little easier. I've been cooking meals, doing laundry, staying home as often as I can. I don't know what more I could do."

Without realizing it, Nathan's movement toward his wife had one primary goal: to prove his adequacy by impacting his wife. Her non-improvement stirred long-denied feelings of emptiness first felt with his father, who pushed his son to succeed, to make his mark, to be a man. Driven by a freshly aroused terror of weightlessness, he felt anger toward his wife and shame toward himself, neither of which he acknowledged, and a powerful urge to feel alive as a man. The pleasures of pornography provided the feelings of masculinity without risking masculine failure. Sexual images on his computer screen could be passively enjoyed without masculine movement.

Pornography worked. An illegitimate goal was reached. Nathan felt good about himself with no need to repent.

Wayne's Story

I understand Nathan, but I did not connect with him. To whatever degree I am broken by an awareness of my own relational sin, to that degree I cannot connect at the deepest level with a man who has little awareness of his relational failure. With Wayne, things were different. We connected as two struggling men who were fighting a similar battle between relational sin and masculine movement. We both realized that our tongues, even when they formed good-sounding words, could be instruments of death.

Wayne, a devoted Christian, loved his wife but often felt resentful of her. He understood that a controlling mother and uninvolved father left him with a powerful longing for a woman to know him and a man to want him. But when life knocked him down and he longed to be known in his fear, his wife either backed away in confused silence or offered encouraging pleasantries.

"Sometimes I get really mad, more ticked off than disappointed," he told me. "She seems to think that if she's just cheerful and bouncy I'll feel better."

"What does your anger make you want to do?" I asked.

"Just get away from her, get busy, eat something, anything to not face how alone I feel. But I know when I do that I'm wanting to feel alive without God. And I'm realizing that I can only *experience* God, to know I'm really alive in Him, by *expressing* God in how I relate, by moving like God toward my wife. It's a battle, but when I do move, when I think more about what's going on in her and how I can represent Christ to her whether or not she responds to me as I want, somehow I feel more solid, and I know I'm alive."

"More centered? Maybe joyful?"

"Not always, but yes. I'm starting to discover something in me that wants my wife to feel safe with me, and appreciated, seen, and wanted." With a slight smile, Wayne added, "Maybe I really am a Christian. I can't imagine finding that desire in me if it weren't for Christ."

This man is in the battle, the real one: not the battle to persuade his wife to fill his void, but the battle to discover and release his masculine longing to reveal Christ's movement toward His people. Wayne fights by moving toward his wife to *hear* her cry, to *remember* God's undeserved grace, and to *look* into her soul until she is visible to him. Then he *moves* with words that reflect his desire to touch her soul with gospel love. He is learning what it takes for his tongue to become an instrument of life. The learning curve is slow, for both of us. But we believe the road we're on leads to life.

—

The battle to become relationally feminine or masculine is engaged when relational sin is recognized and war is declared, civil war: on one side is the flesh obsessed with its own demands, and on the other side is the renewed human spirit that desires to enjoy God by revealing His relational nature to others.

It is only when war is declared that the power of relational sin is truly felt. Defeat seems certain. The urge to look after oneself is too strong to resist. Victory, relating as feminine women or masculine men, is beyond reach.

And it is then that the sincerely struggling Christian cries out, "Oh wretched fool that I am, I am not who I long to be! I'm at the end of my rope, empty of goodness and broken by sin. Who can form me into the relational image of Christ? I desire nothing more than to be fully alive, to speak life words to others, not death words, to make known the wonder of God's relational glory by the miraculous way I relate. From the depths of my broken heart, I cry, 'Have mercy on me, a relational sinner.'"

War is declared when relational sin is exposed. Inevitable defeat stirs desperate dependence. Christ in me is my only hope for relational glory. It is here that *the search for our center* begins, the search to discover the life of God in the soul of a woman or man, the life that can energize and direct the way we relate and the words we speak.

17

THERE IS A CENTER

Our Mistake Is Indifference to Its Existence

In his passion to set right a disjointed universe, God broke open his own heart in love. God's center—the love between the Father and the Son—is now offered as our center; God's heart breaks open so as to include even the worst and most hopeless among us.

Because of this questing and self-emptying divine love, we become friends of God, sharers in the communion of the Trinity. That is the essence of Christianity. Everything else is commentary.

This is the first path of holiness: finding the center which is divine love.

Robert Barron[1]

I am writing this book to answer one question: *What did God have in mind when He made us male and female?* He does everything for His own glory, to display Himself for the benefit of others. So why this?

Each of us, as a man or a woman, is called by the gospel to find ourselves by losing ourselves in God's love story. It strikes me, therefore, that the question I am asking is at least important enough to take seriously.

---

1. Robert Barron, *The Strangest Way* (Maryknoll, NY: Orbis Press, 2002), 31, 32, and 34, respectively.

If you have hung with me this far, you know at least two things (and I hope more!). One: I strongly believe every one of us should be asking this question and looking for answers. I think it's that important. Two: I believe the Bible answers this question we all should be asking.

God's consuming and passionate purpose is to reveal Himself, to give Himself to us as the one community of persons we were created to most enjoy and also to resemble and reveal. The more traditional way of saying this is to say that God does everything He does for His own glory.

God made us male and female for His glory. As women and men, we glorify God by relating to others in this world in a manner that reveals something both staggering and stunning about the way God relates, something far beyond anything we could be or even imagine on our own.

What we are designed to reveal about God is something that, as gendered image-bearers, we were wired to uniquely enjoy and reveal. Because Jesus fully revealed the Father by the way He related as a human being, the Spirit is now forming us into "little Christs," feminine women who reveal God's beautiful invitation to the divine dance, and masculine men who reveal the beautiful movement of God that makes possible our invitation to the dance.

I am praying that what you read in these pages is drawing you to become more fully alive as a woman or man by the way you relate. I hope you're giving these ideas serious thought.

But I can also imagine four other reactions to what I'm saying. I can imagine them clearly because each one has flitted through my mind.

First, *this is impossible.* "I can't live like that. It's too dangerous, too difficult. Open myself as a woman with no guarantee that I'll be treated well? Rape comes in various forms, you know." "What you're suggesting offends me. Forget about living to be successful and recognized as a man who's really good at something? And instead move toward people with no greater purpose than to bless them at any cost to me? No way. That's stupid!"

Second, *this is impractical.* "It's too vague. I hear what you're saying and I am drawn to the idea of relating well, but I'm not at all clear on exactly what it would mean to relate in some feminine or masculine way." "I'm more comfortable with a plan that tells me what to do, how to manage my life so that things have their best chance of working as they're supposed to. I prefer formulas and techniques that I can follow, not vague, mysterious ideas that I don't know how to apply."

Third, *this is irrelevant*. "To be blunt, and you might think it's unchristian, but I have more pressing things to deal with than whether I am a spiritually forming feminine woman. One of my kids has a pretty severe learning disability. And making financial ends meet is not easy." "I'm more worried about abortion and drugs and the economy and terrorists than being masculine." "I know what you're saying. I know it's important to let others know what God is like by how I treat them, but when you're in a burning house you've got to put the fire out before you have a meaningful chat with your neighbor."

Fourth, *this is unnecessary*. "I already am a committed Christian. I do want to live for God's glory. I've been on mission trips, I lead a small group Bible study, I live a moral and responsible life, I love Jesus, and I do my best to love my family and friends well. I don't mean to be unkind, but all these ideas about relational femininity and relational masculinity feel like side issues." "You're just confusing me with religious-sounding inessentials. I'll continue to do my best to live a good Christian life, believing what's true and doing what's right. I'm more interested in changing the world than changing myself."

If you find yourself responding to what you're reading in any of these four ways, consider this: Christians who aim too low never discover the center of their souls where God lives. They never know the overwhelming desire to be spiritually formed so that they reveal Christ to others at any cost to themselves. And they never experience the power to be fully alive as women and men for the glory of God.

Until divine love becomes our center, until love is our organizing principle for living and our compelling energy for relating, we will live to protect ourselves from others or to preserve ourselves through others.

It was Thomas Aquinas, the great Catholic theologian, who once said that love is willing the good of another, and not willing our own good through another—except through Jesus Christ.

Think what it would mean to literally bring God's kingdom to earth as Jesus did, to reveal divinity in humanity, to be (as some call it) "deified."

When Godfrey Diekmann, a highly respected church historian, was ninety-two, Professor Robert Barron asked him a question.

"Godfrey, if you were young again and could mount the barricades, what would you fight for in the church today?"

Although Diekmann was very old, his mind was razor sharp and his heart was burning hot. As Barron tells the story, "Bringing his cane down on my knee, he said, without a moment's hesitation, 'deification.'"[2]

The early church fathers called it *theiosis*. The Latin word that translates the Greek *theiosis* is *deificatio*, or "becoming divine and revealing the divine nature in human relating." Listen to Jesus as He talks with His Father: "I have given them the glory you gave me" (John 17:22 NLT). What glory does He mean? The glory of divinity that the second Person of the Trinity knew from all eternity? Or was it the *relational* glory given to Jesus at His incarnation, the power of the fully human Jesus, the still and always fully divine Christ, to reveal the Father's way of relating by the way He related *as a human being*?

It is that glory Jesus gives us, the glory that creates the God-glorifying opportunity to reveal divinity in humanity so that we "may be one" as the Father and Son are one (see John 17:22). This is the gospel, the gospel of deification, our becoming "little Christs," women and men who reveal the life of the Trinity by the way we relate to each other.

We are intended for more: living fully alive in relational femininity and relational masculinity for God's glory.

- *Is it impossible?* Yes, if there is no divine life filling our deepest soul, if Jesus did not really give us the glory His Father gave Him.
- *Is it impractical?* In one sense, of course. There are no steps to follow, no formula that makes clear precisely what we should do in any relational encounter. But we can learn to live in the rhythm of the divine energy that motivated everything Jesus said and did.
- *Is it irrelevant?* Again, yes—if our goal is to find everything we were created to enjoy in only what this world can provide. If, however, our deepest desire is to be made holy, then nothing is more relevant to our joy than becoming fully alive as feminine women and masculine men by living a new way from our new center.
- *Is it unnecessary?* If our spiritual formation matters to us, our opportunity to live from our center is indispensable; it is a gift to treasure.

2. Ibid., 29.

There is a center, and it is not me. It is Christ in me. "Being holy, burning with the fire of God's own life, is the point."[3] Rock guitarist Eric Clapton once remarked that he plays his instrument best when his instrument plays him. And we play our lives best when our divine center plays us.

As Christians, we have been given a new center, the other-centered passion of God's Spirit, no longer the self-centered energy of our flesh. As Barron puts it, "our first responsibility is to welcome it."[4] But if we think living a new way from a new center is impossible, impractical, irrelevant, or unnecessary, we will ignore the gift.

Every woman who, above everything else she desires, longs to welcome Christ's invitation to dance with the Trinity and to offer that same invitation to others by the way she relates, will search for her center with the eagerness of a shepherd searching for a lost sheep. She will realize that there is a divine center lodged in her soul that can empower her to come alive in relational femininity for the glory of God.

And every man who, wanting more than recognition and respect, desires to be radically transformed by Christ's movement into his soul and to reveal that same movement to others by the way he relates, will search for his center the way the prodigal's father kept looking for his son. He will know that there is a divine center fixed in his soul that can release God-like movement into others as he comes alive with relational masculinity for the glory of God.

How can we be indifferent to the divine center in each of us? How can we long for less than living as men and women in all that we are for the pleasure of the One who made us all that we are? How can we value anything above the relational glory of our graciously inviting and sacrificially moving God, a glory that is our center, our opportunity to really live meaningfully now—and fully forever?

There is a center. The center of the universe, the love that eternally flows back and forth between the Father and the Son, the love that is the bridge for their inseparable connection, is now our center. Our center is our new heart, where the Spirit of the Father and the Son lives.

3. Ibid.
4. Ibid., 32.

But it is hidden beneath our futile efforts to numb our core terrors—invisibility in a woman, weightlessness in a man—beneath our foolish self-centered, self-protective, self-displaying way of relating that never draws us together in Trinity-like connection on the bridge.

It's time to search for our center in Christ. The search is difficult. It will be painful, perhaps agonizingly slow. Our shallow comfort will need to be forfeited. The way is dark, the path is bumpy, and the road is narrow, but life awaits us on the Bridge of Connection.

18

SEARCH FOR YOUR CENTER

It is no longer I who live, but Christ who lives in me.

Galatians 2:20

What Jesus implies is that he has opened for his followers a new depth of existence, a new center, that cannot be touched even when the whole of what we customarily call the "self" has been destroyed.

Robert Barron[1]

No storm can shake my inmost calm while to that rock I'm clinging.

Quaker Hymn

The central paradox of the spiritual path is that in striving to transcend the self, we actually build it up; our holy solutions invariably calcify into grotesque casts of ego. Getting real is harder than we've been led to believe. The real gift, the real grace, is surrender, and surrender almost always feels like a defeat and a failure.

Tim Farrington[2]

1. Robert Barron, *The Strangest Way* (Mary Knoll, NY: Orbis Books, 2002), 45.
2. Tim Farrington, *A Hell of Mercy* (New York: Harper One, 2009), 115–16.

The memory is vivid, still warmly present in my mind even though shrouded in the fog of good times long gone. On cold winter mornings near Philadelphia, in a quiet village called Plymouth Meeting where to this day Quakers still worship in a historic meeting house that stands in the town center, as an eight-year-old boy I would wake to an alarm clock set to a half hour before mother would put breakfast on the table. I would quickly brush my teeth, dress for school (except for socks and shoes), grab my pillow and a couple of Superman comic books, and then stretch out on the green tiled living room floor with my head on the pillow, my comics in hand, and my bare feet carefully positioned two to three inches in front of the heat register. It never occurred to me someone had to pay for the warm air.

For twenty minutes, I would begin my day by reading stories of the red-caped hero as he foiled the evil plots of bad guys and with his power and goodness made everything right in the world (at least in Metropolis) while my toes happily wiggled in the warm air that didn't cost me a dime.

Bill, my older brother, would still be in bed. He always arrived at the breakfast table a few minutes after Dad had thanked God for the food, always with his teeth unbrushed, never fully dressed, and usually in a not-too-good mood. Bill's grumpiness amused me and let me feel both sorry for him and superior to him. Life was good, just as I wanted it to be.

Every few minutes I would put my comic down, look to my left, and see my aproned mother scrambling eggs, frying bacon, pouring orange juice, and dutifully refilling my dad's almost empty coffee cup. And my father, who was unfailingly in his place at the breakfast table before I arrived in the living room with pillow and Superman, would be reading the Bible, a big, black, Scofield Reference Edition King James Bible.

I didn't know the Hebrew word then, but if I had, I would have been whispering it to myself every morning: *shalom*, everything is as it should be. I had recently given my life to Jesus. Now He was giving me the life I wanted. God was good. Christianity was a good deal. The Christian life was a good way to go. I had no reason to think that this *shalom* might not continue.

Sixty years have passed. I now wake up every morning to an uncommonly blessed life, to loving family, good friends, and meaningful activity, and an occasional round of adequately played golf. Some days, of course, are not so good. Life happens. On August 12, 2011, Rachael drove me to the hospital where Dr. Neff removed cancer from my liver. He is a skillful doctor. Surgery went well. I now wake up every morning cancer free, with medically controlled hypertension and only a few pounds of extra weight. Life is good. Now I know the word *shalom*, but . . . I can't quite say it. Why?

I don't know a Hebrew word that means "not *shalom*," but if I did, it would occur to me most mornings, accompanied by an unsolicited inner groaning, a longing that seems relentlessly inconsolable, even on good days when I drive to the golf course instead of the hospital. I can't seem to escape the reality I never saw as a child: *nothing* is as it should be, not exactly. Too many things are exactly as they *shouldn't* be. And nothing that's good today is guaranteed to be good tomorrow. A threatening cloud hovers on the horizon of every sun-filled day.

I thought by now, nearing seventy years of age and alive in Christ for more than sixty of those years, I would be climbing out of bed every morning not to enjoy warm air blowing over my feet but rather singing, "This is the day the Lord has made, and I will rejoice and be glad in it" (see Ps. 118:24). Some days I do. More often I don't. On my worst days, I want to pull the covers over my head and not get up at all.

Why? Am I depressed? Am I a glass-half-empty kind of guy, the proverbial Gloomy Gus, a Christian man who somehow manages to be more miserable than grateful in the middle of a much-blessed life? Am I diagnosable, in need of my own kind of professional help? Some friends think so. My physician recently insisted I fill a prescription for Zoloft, an antidepressant. The small bottle sits unopened on the bathroom counter. Am I living in denial?

I have no problem with Christians taking mood-elevating medication. A close friend of mine swallows a dose of Prozac every day. I judge him no more than I judge another close friend who every day takes insulin for diabetes. Prozac frees my chemically depressed friend through chemicals that help him to better fight the battle raging in every Christian's soul, the battle between flesh-energized self-obsession and Spirit-releasing God obsession, and to more fully live in the strength of his hope-filled center, where Christ lives, where *shalom* can be tasted.

I don't take my Zoloft because I don't believe I suffer from clinical depression. But I do struggle with anti-*shalom*, with biblical groaning (see Romans 8) that every self-aware Christian will feel until the day Jesus returns and makes everything right—in us and in the world. I regard my angst, which sometimes expresses itself in acedia, not as a symptom of pathology but as evidence of growing maturity, of facing the reality within me and in the world that something is wrong with everything.

I also see my angst as a doorway to the search for my divine center, the same center that was in Jesus when He lived in this disjointed world. The opportunity to push open the door doesn't always excite me. There are days, and more of them as I get older, when I shower, dress, and dream of grabbing a pillow and Superman comics and letting warm air blow over my naked feet. I long for *shalom*. I want it now.

But those eight-year-old days were not *shalom*. The peace I enjoyed then was the product of naive immaturity, perfectly appropriate for a young child to feel, but wrong for a grown-up to never move beyond.

As I groan inwardly and wait eagerly, I have the opportunity to live as a man, to *hear* the groaning of another person living without *shalom*; to *remember* the God who is always moving to create a taste of *shalom* and always inviting us to the soon-coming banquet; to *look* into another's life to identify what's getting in the way of experiencing the joy of released femininity or masculinity; and to *move* into another's life with the love-releasing life of God.

In order to seize my opportunity to relate as a God-revealing man, I must first *find my center*. I must cut through the angst, feel the sorrow of a half-empty cup, and let my groans provide momentum to search for the down payment of divine life that is already in me, the life of Christ Himself that can empower me to relate like Him, to live in relational masculinity on both good days and bad, on the golf course or in a hospital bed.

If I don't live from my center, then even though I preach a sermon, hug my wife, write a book, counsel a friend, lead a conference, enjoy my grand-kids, or sing in church, I will do nothing as a man. I will not be relating as a man fully alive for the glory of God.

―――

When a man opens his eyes and sees a pre-*shalom* world in which he is not relating with true masculinity, he will face a crossroad: either remain dead in self-obsession or search for his God-alive center, a center that when discovered will slowly transform him into the man of movement God made him to be.

When a woman looks into her heart and sees a relationally dangerous world that she is protecting herself against by closing her soul, she will respond in one of only two possible ways: either she will remain closed in the coffin of self-obsession or she will search for her God-alive center, a center that when found will gradually transform her into a God-revealing invitational woman.

A man's center is flowing with the beauty of divine movement. A woman's center is radiant with the beauty of divine invitation. In his deepest core, every Christian man is masculine. In her deepest core, every Christian woman is feminine. If we're to live fully alive in relational masculinity or relational femininity, we must live from our center.

Before we can live from our center, however, we must find it. But how?

19

Preparing to Live Fully Alive

Catch the Vision and Count the Cost

I devoted myself to search for understanding and to explore by wisdom everything being done under heaven. I soon discovered that God has dealt a tragic existence to the human race.

Ecclesiastes 1:13 NLT

For the creation was subjected to futility. . . . And not only the creation, but we ourselves, who have the firstfruits of the Spirit, groan inwardly as we wait eagerly.

Romans 8:20, 23

Whether it is a damp, drizzly November in my soul; whenever I find myself involuntarily pausing before coffin warehouses, and bringing up the rear of every funeral I meet; and especially whenever my hypos [gloom that lurks in the background of one's life] get such an upper hand of me, that it requires a strong moral principle to prevent me from deliberately stepping into the street and methodically knocking people's hats off—then I account it high time to get to the sea as soon as I can. This is my substitute for pistol and ball.

Ishmael (Herman Melville)[1]

1. Herman Melville, *Moby Dick* (New York: Barnes and Noble Classics, 2003), 27.

Who today lives fully for the glory of God? Is it even possible? What would it look like to live that way? Is such a lofty goal even in our sight? If not, why not?

Do we not realize that a woman fully alive in her femininity will know a joy that comes to her in no other way? Is it clear to us that a woman alive in relational femininity will be occupied not with her rights as a woman but with her undeserved privileges, that she will not obsess over a needy demand to be valued and wanted but will gratefully claim her opportunity to reveal the One she most values and wants?

And have we failed to understand that a man fully alive in his masculinity will not be frozen by fear in his relationships but will rather be released into love? Do we not excitedly believe that a masculine man will not retreat from the dangers of relational intimacy? He will not be controlled by even strong fear of being exposed as a man with little relational weight, of being seen as a man who does not know how to draw close to anyone. A manly man will gladly respond to the call to meaningfully connect with God and with others: his wife, his children, his parents, and his friends. Do we not know that a God-obsessed man will move toward others even when he has little understanding of how to connect with anyone, that he will (often with unfelt confidence) move in faith that he is moving with divine weight, with the power of godly impact?

As I write this book, the prayer consumes me that we all catch the vision of what it would mean to live as fully alive women and men. And I realize that we will not embrace and pursue this vision until we agree that achieving it is worth any cost.

Never have we lived in a culture less captured by the deep beauty of womanhood, less fragrant with the aroma of God-revealing femininity.

And never have we seen a culture less relaxed in the presence of manhood, less anchored in the solidness of God-revealing masculinity.

But there is a culture uniquely called and powerfully equipped to make known the beauty of a suffering invitational God through women and to display the beauty of a sacrificially moving God through men: *the church, the community of God on earth, is designed to reveal the community of God in heaven.*

But it's not happening, not as powerfully as the gospel makes possible. Too often, the church is known for its commitment to social justice more than its commitment to social intimacy. Heated debate over women's roles and men's authority continues while relational tensions remain hidden and unaddressed. We settle for congeniality when God calls us to connection. Functional relationships keep the church moving with programs, preaching, and projects that lack spiritual power. Trinity-like relating requires human brokenness and divine power. The vision has not yet been caught and the cost has not yet been counted.

Whatever Else She May Be

Picture a woman who represents all Christian women today, standing on one end of the Bridge of Connection. Listen closely and you will hear her asking, "Will anyone come? Will anyone cross the bridge to be with me? Will anyone see me and want whom they see? Will a man see beauty that he desires, a precious beauty to cherish, not a cheap beauty that he will want to use for his own pleasure? Is there within me a beauty to be seen? Or am I invisible, a woman in whom there is nothing to see and desire? Will I forever live unseen and unwanted?"

She is afraid. Fear controls her. She feels needy and weak, vulnerable to intolerable hurt. But she hides her fear. She comes across to others as together, or perhaps demanding, or maybe even cheerful. This woman is obsessed with herself. She is aware of no greater good than being seen and wanted, her beauty visible to others.

Through no one's fault but her own, she is slowly sinking into the quicksand of self-preoccupation. She lives in slavery to the terror of invisibility, relational death, a tragic existence in isolation. She needs compassion—not centered on her suffering, but on her selfishness. She needs the compassion of grace. She is trapped behind walls of her own making.

This woman sees no option but to protect herself from further pain and to prove herself desirable. She therefore parades whatever style of relating hides her fear and reveals virtues and talents that win approval. Her strongest felt desires are those that grow in the soil of self-obsession, desires that inevitably become demands for satisfaction to which she feels entitled.

This woman lives with her arms folded and with her soul closed, uninviting and impassable. But she stays busy, searching for satisfaction that never comes. "It is an unhappy business that God has given to the children of man to be busy with" (Eccles. 1:13), a tragic existence that she desperately tries to rise above.

She may be a home-schooling mom devoted to her kids and happily involved with her husband or a capable career woman who relishes the challenge to succeed in a man's world. She might direct women's ministry in her church, organize Sunday morning greeters, or serve as senior pastor. This woman could be either an aggressively content or a frantically desperate single woman; perhaps she is a medical professional, a well-heeled socialite, or a dutiful Christian wife who remains intentionally unknown to her husband. Or she might be enjoying a satisfying marriage that is equally available to a woman without Christ.

Perhaps she can no longer endure a difficult marriage and files for divorce from her abusive husband. She then may feel the scorn of her church for failing to be submissive while she draws strength from the applause of sympathetic friends. And she wonders whether God is disgusted with her refusal to submit or is clapping in rhythm with her friends' applause.

Whatever else she may be, she is not a feminine woman.

Only a vision of what it would mean to be fully alive in relational femininity for God's glory will reveal the presence and power of her relational sin. This vision will arouse a holy desire to die to her unfeminine way of relating and to be resurrected by God's Spirit into the relational life of God-revealing femininity.

Only then will she fruitfully, without the pride of self-contempt, cry, "Oh, what a miserable woman I am. I fall so terribly short of the purpose for which I've been created. I'm a female but I'm not feminine. Who will lift me out of this swamp of self-obsession, from this tragic existence controlled by fear, ruled by self, and destined for meaninglessness?"

Only the power of the relational God who moves into our lives and invites us to move into His can provide the will to count the cost and find the courage to descend into the dark regions of the spiritually forming life—where this woman has no one and nothing but Christ, and then discovers that He is enough.

Whatever Else He May Be

Imagine a man standing on the other side of the bridge, a man who represents Christian men today. Never loud enough for another to hear, and barely loud enough to hear himself, the man asks, "Does anyone respect me? Does anyone notice what I have to offer and value what I can provide? Is there a woman who realizes I have substance that deserves appreciation and not criticism? Do I come across as weak, driven by ego needs, in need of help? Does no one rest in my presence, eager to draw close enough to me to receive what I can give? Or am I a male without substance, a man who lacks relational weight, a man who is capable of making only superficial impact on people? Will I forever live unworthy of respect?"

No matter how strong he appears, this man is scared. Fear drives his movement and directs his energies toward meeting his own needs. He lives to hide his inadequacy and to display whatever wins him recognition. He lives alone, behind walls of self-protection and self-enhancement, a slave to his own desperate demand to be someone that he fears he is not.

But he puts his game face on, like a nervous quarterback before kickoff. He backs away from any level of involvement that risks exposure of his relational incompetence, and gets busy with other things. "It is an unhappy business that God has given to the children of man to be busy with" (Eccles. 1:13), a tragic existence that he covers over with whatever creates the illusion of meaning and the feeling of power.

He could be a young businessman quickly climbing the ladder in corporate America. I can see him playing ball with his son and taking his little girl on a daddy-daughter date. He may be a respected Christian, active in his church, a popular Sunday school teacher, a leading elder, or a senior pastor. Perhaps he is a military man, strong and in charge, with stars on his uniform, his shoulders squared, and standing tall. Or he could be a leader on Wall Street or in government.

This man might be a devoted husband, a Christian who believes it is his calling to protect his wife, not to pursue her; to pursue only the Lord, never journeying together with his wife. How sad the condition of a man who feels safely hidden and publicly alive, a man who remains in hiding and relieves his boredom and fills his emptiness with secret sexual activities or stepped-up dedication to career success—or perhaps to greater spiritual disciplines designed to thicken his godly veneer.

Whatever else he may be, he is not a masculine man.

Only a vision of whom he could become, a man fully alive in relational masculinity, will convict him of how dead he is and excite him with a holy desire to die to unmasculine relating, no matter how painful it might be, and to be raised by God into the new way of the Spirit, into the relational life of God-revealing masculinity.

Only then will he cry in hope-filled brokenness, "Oh, what a failure I am as an image-bearing man. The cross of Christ means little to me beyond fire insurance. I have not been greatly changed by the gospel. I am a male who is not masculine. I do not reveal God's character by the way I relate. Who can rescue me from the fear that controls how I move, from my tragic existence as an empty man who fills himself by using others, who lives a life that makes no eternal difference?"

Only the power of a weighty God who moves with impact and a compassionate God who invites relationship can supply what this man needs to descend into the terrifying regions of the spiritually-forming life where he is stripped of everything but Christ—and then realizes he is fully clothed.

Believe what the gospel makes possible. Imagine what could be. Divine beauty lives in the center of every woman who knows Jesus, the beauty of the God who invites us into His community. Divine beauty lives in the center of every man in whom the Spirit of Jesus lives, the beauty of the God who moved into our neighborhood with the power to make us a community.

But that divine beauty lives only in our center. In every other region of my being, fallen ugliness rules. Apart from God's Spirit, I am relentlessly determined to reach two goals that my flesh values: to live well according to values I naturally embrace so that my life goes well according to preferences that honor me, and to depend on whatever means are at my disposal and under my control that promise to relieve both discomfort brought on by difficult circumstances and emotional suffering that is occasioned by unmet desires.

Those two goals never change. They never weaken. They never lose their appeal. Without new life from Christ, I would live my life pursuing those two purposes, and this life would prove to be a living death that ends in dead death—fully conscious but eternally dead.

Wretched man that I am! Wretched woman or man that you are! Who will deliver us from death to life, to living as God-revealing women and men?

Herman Melville's character Ishmael believed that when all he could feel was inconsolable despair in the presence of death and angry frustration on his journey through life, it was time to get to the sea, to find the river of life. Perhaps he didn't realize that out of his heart could flow living water. Ishmael didn't know it, but "getting to the sea" really means coming to Jesus and following wherever He leads.

Jesus spoke, not of getting to Ishmael's sea, but of walking a narrow road that leads to the water of life, a road that would free us to live with no greater longing than to know God and make Him known by how we relate as men and women.

He called it a narrow road that could only be entered through a narrow gate. And He warned us that not many find it. The road to life is less traveled for a reason. The pursuit of gendered relating can seem futile, requiring apparently pointless effort that seems to change nothing, or very little very slowly. We never live fully alive in this world. Opposition is strong, strong from the outside and stronger from the inside.

The world squeezes us into its way of thinking about gender and leaves us either defensively committed to unthreatening ideas or proudly open to self-enhancing ideas. The devil deceives us into believing that the way of relating that feels right in the moment *is* right. And our flesh buys the lies and prompts us to live accordingly.

Who can free us from the persuasive power of this unholy trinity of the world, the devil, and the flesh? We know the Christian answer: Jesus Christ! But *how* does He rescue us? "Just pray about it." "Don't miss church." "Trust God." Glib answers like these won't do. We know God is for us and that He is stronger than our enemy. But the forces lined up against us can feel stronger than God.

What, then, is the narrow road we must walk if we are to discover the power to live as relationally alive men and women? And how do we walk it?

PART IV

BECOMING FULLY ALIVE

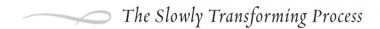 *The Slowly Transforming Process*

Our task is nothing less than this: to achieve within human life the love that is a dim reflection of the life of God.

Gilbert C. Meilaender[1]

From conception, every child is a unique and distinctively gendered bearer of God's image. Since Eden, however, every one of us born into this world (except the One conceived in a virgin's womb) arrives with a dominant inclination to discover both our uniqueness and our gendered identity through our own resourcefulness. We enter life dead to God and alive to ourselves.

But then, from the moment of rebirth in Christ, every man and woman is made alive: alive *to* God, *for* God, and *with* God. God's Spirit, the Spirit of relational holiness, lives in the center of every Christian woman, energizing her to relate in a way that reveals the invitational God who opens Himself to eagerly welcome all who hear His call and enter His community. That

1. Stanley J. Grenz, *The Social God and the Relational Self* (Louisville, KY: Westminster John Knox Press, 2001), 32.

same Spirit makes His home in the center of every Christian man, empowering him to relate in a way that reveals the moving God who passionately longs to pour His life-giving love into every opened heart.

But there is a problem. Powerful forces that oppose God and are in us from conception (what J. I. Packer calls an anti-God virus) convincingly argue that in this relationally dangerous world it is wise to look out for ourselves and to choose a safe path, to walk a comfortably broad road. But there is only one road that leads to the community we were designed to enjoy, and in its enjoyment, find ourselves. It's a narrow road that not many find.

And now, the final question: How does the Trinity's perfectly holy and thoroughly happy relationship release feminine life in Jesus-following women and masculine life in Jesus-following men so that they meet on the Bridge of Connection?

20

THE JOURNEY BEGINS

From Female to Feminine, from Male to Masculine

Howling one's head off may actually be a more mature and realistic response to reality than the elaborate social skills of many adults. With the latter so frightfully focused on grinning and bearing their way through life, perhaps babies are the ones to whom God has entrusted the important work of doing the crying for the whole world.

[Christian counselors too often] subtly but clearly convey the message that every believer should exhibit a certain level of emotional well-being (or at least show steady progress in that direction), and if anyone does not yield to their ministry, then that person's faith becomes suspect.

If our gospel is not one that, like Job's, will stand up to the prolonged test of having absolutely no circumstantial evidence of worldly success, then it is a gospel of straw. It is a gospel founded on appearances, not on the cross of Christ.

Mike Mason[1]

In these final chapters, I wrestle with a message that I would rather not present and that you would rather not hear, a message that's difficult to

1. Mike Mason, *The Gospel According to Job* (Wheaton, IL: Crossway, 1994), 186, 173, and 146, respectively.

believe because of the way we naturally think. When I'm thinking right, however, it's the message I most want to present because it is clearly taught in the Bible and lays out the only path to the life that every woman and every man most want to live. Remember: the beginning of the gospel is bad news, the center of the gospel is good news, and the end of the gospel story is deliriously good—forever!

Life As It Is

Has God really "dealt a tragic existence to the human race" (Eccles. 1:13 NLT)? The writer of Ecclesiastes seemed to think so. But what is tragic in the life of someone who is blessed with good family and friends, good health and income, and good talents with plenty of opportunity to display them? Perhaps Solomon, the assumed author of this almost-depressing book, was thinking only of starving people in a famine-cursed country, or citizens oppressed by a cruel dictator, or out-of-work people surrounded by friends with good jobs, or patients on medication designed to relieve their pain as they await death.

But he wasn't, though certainly he had unfortunate folks in mind. For some reason, this powerful, wealthy, wise man who had unlimited opportunities for pleasure of every kind felt prompted to "search out by wisdom" (1:13) what everyone's life, especially his own, was all about. But he couldn't "find out what God has done from the beginning to the end" (3:11).

The Hebrew word translated "find out" means to think hard, to analyze, to figure out, to make sense of, and to comprehend by study. Why did one good friend's teenage son die suddenly in a car crash? Why did the daughter of other good friends of mine die after a long illness that doctors believed might be cured? Why are two good pastors I know going through such hard times with their church? Solomon's search to understand life ended in the cul-de-sac of an evil that he had "seen under the sun," an evil that "lies heavy on mankind" (6:1).

I remember telling a Sunday school class years ago that every honest person, everyone who takes the blinders off and sees life as it really is in human experience, will be required to choose one of only three options: commit suicide, go mad, or trust God. And those who choose option three must trust God radically and repeatedly, in even the worst of times. One man in the class, a wealthy businessman with a beautiful wife and two high-achieving, healthy, and responsible kids, stared at me with puzzled disdain. God had dealt him a tragic existence? What was tragic about his life? Everything was good. I suppose he thought I was mad with severe depression or angry nihilism, or maybe I happened that Sunday to be in a really bad mood. But by the time we finish Part IV, we will all be able, I pray, to see that what Solomon said is true: God has dealt us a tragic existence, no matter what our assortment of blessings or troubles might be.

But we will also realize that seeing, feeling, and embracing what is truly tragic about life in this world presents an opportunity, our best and only opportunity, to come alive with the power to love as feminine women and masculine men. And it is the exercise of that power, the power to love others for the purpose of revealing the God we love who first loved us, that brings with it the deep, solid, and anchoring joy of fully living for the glory of our God.

Seeing the Road Ahead

Look back to the three quotes that appear at the start of this chapter. These words by Mike Mason nudge me further along on a road I sometimes reluctantly walk toward a destination I eagerly anticipate. And these words (along with those of Solomon) stir up hard questions.

Howling one's head off represents movement toward maturity? Why?

Agonizing over losses, over blessings that are no longer mine to enjoy, or not yet mine to fully enjoy, is somehow good? How?

A baby's cry sends a message to laughing adults that they need to hear? What is it?

If truly living in either our femininity or masculinity requires that we face a reality that makes us miserable, wouldn't it be smarter to keep our blinders on and live in pleasant denial, to be content as superficially feminine women or masculine men?

As we ask these questions, I think we need to listen to James. He was a younger brother of Jesus, which means that he literally grew up with God. I wonder if as a teenager and on into His twenties Jesus was already showing signs that He was a man of sorrows and acquainted with grief (see Isa. 53:3). I don't know, but I do know that after hanging around Jesus for several decades, James said some disturbing things.

Here are two of James's sentences that at first glance sound like melancholy overstatement, perhaps the product of a morbid mind: "Be wretched and mourn and weep. Let your laughter be turned to mourning and your joy to gloom" (James 4:9).

Paul comes across as no more cheerful than James when, after looking at the quality of his own life as a Christian, he wrote, "Wretched man that I am" (Rom. 7:24). But then he left the gloom in Romans 7 behind and moved into the freedom and joy of God's love in Romans 8. *And yet even then he was still groaning!*

Over what? Failure still plagued him. Paul never claimed that he no longer sinned. And he knew that life in this world required him to wait for the full enjoyment of what Jesus had already accomplished. Paul walked a narrow road with emptiness and brokenness as close companions, right up until he was beheaded—and then he danced as he never had before.

I listen to James and Paul and hear them telling me that I will *worship well* only when I *groan deep*, and that if we're to be formed into feminine women and masculine men, to become who we most want to be, we'll be required to cry the tears we most fear. Groaning worship and tear-stained transformation: Are they really necessary? Is that God's plan?

Must the narrow road to feminine or masculine life be *that* narrow? Isn't the Christian life a little less drastic and easier than *that*, and not nearly so tragic? Bonhoeffer declared that when Christ calls someone to follow Him, He bids him come and die. Did he miss what Jesus meant when He invited us to come to Him and *rest*? Did life in Nazi Germany cloud Bonhoeffer's vision of an appealing Christian life? Or did a tragic existence reveal loftier truth?

I want James and Paul to contradict Bonhoeffer and tell me pleasant things, to explain to me that Jesus wants to give me a bed to rest on rather than a yoke to bear. I want to believe that I'm already quite masculine and that becoming even more masculine requires only enjoyable effort, perhaps time in a men's group and the practice of a few spiritual disciplines.

Then James continues: good news is coming! To people drowning in the misery of feeling empty and falling short, James says, "Humble yourselves before the Lord, *and he will exalt you*" (James 4:10, emphasis added). I think Hosea, the prophet God led into a miserable marriage, understood this long before James said it when he wrote, "In their distress [God's] people [will] earnestly seek [God]" (Hos. 5:15).

Along with more recent old-timers such as St. John of the Cross, who wrote about dark nights, John Bunyan, who caught a glimpse of the narrow road while spending twelve years in prison because he loved Jesus, and C. S. Lewis, who worried that the more he knew God the less he might like Him, and along with a few new-timers like Mike Mason, I hear Hosea and Paul and James telling us that deep joy emerges only in deep sorrow, that real femininity and masculinity develop in the tragic existence of felt futility and owned failures, of significant relational pain.

I'm more compelled than drawn to move toward a difficult conclusion: *living fully alive in femininity or masculinity is possible only to the degree that we die—fully dead—to whatever gets in the way.*

Given God's penchant for turning our preferred notions of how best to live upside down (He calls it repentance) and for opening our eyes to clearly see what lifts us up only after He opens our eyes to painfully see what drags us down (He calls it brokenness), I'm not surprised that the road He tells me will lead to the life I want is not one that I find immediately appealing.

I believe His plan is good, but none of us will be happily convinced it's good until we're further along the narrow road He commands us to walk. But I can tell you this: delicious tastes of God's goodness are available as we travel, much like refreshment stands that mark the path laid out for marathon runners.

No refreshment stand, of course, represents the finish line. More sweat and fatigue and nearly unbearable cramps are in store before we finish the race. C. S. Lewis put it this way: "Our Father refreshes us on the journey with some pleasant inns, but will not encourage us to mistake them for home."[2]

But still we do. "Ah, I've met God," we say. "I feel His presence. Life is no longer tragic. I enjoy His blessings. Brokenness is behind me. My void is filled. Further repentance is rarely necessary. I've arrived. I'm home. My life is a tragic existence? That's not how I see it. I'm blessed. I'm healed. I'm really quite mature. It's my immature friends and my difficult spouse who cause all the problems."

2. C. S. Lewis, *The Problem of Pain* (New York: MacMillan, 1962), 115.

When we make that mistake, we settle down in soul-numbing comfort as we amble along on a pleasantly broad road of enjoyed blessings, unseen failures, and discounted troubles. And we don't realize how far short of God's relational glory we continue to fall by living as unfeminine women and unmasculine men. *That* is a tragedy.

I offer part 4 of this book to encourage travelers on the narrow road to stay on it, no matter how narrow it gets, no matter how painfully what we wrongly call "life" is squeezed out of us. To those still happily skipping through life on the broad road of imagined maturity I say: only one road leads to the life you were created and called to live, the life of joyfully connecting to God and gladly offering connection to others, and that road is narrow, but profoundly good!

Join me now as I map the narrow road that, through the unhappy business and tragic existence of life, will transform us into God-revealing feminine women and masculine men. Thanks to Jesus, real life is now ours to live. It's not an easy life, but it's a good life. For a Christian, it's the best life available until heaven, the only life worth living in this world. Don't settle for less. The glory of the God we serve is revealed through women and men who are alive with the relational glory of Jesus. Nothing matters more.

21

LET THE SLOW RACE BEGIN

And let us run with endurance the race God has set before us.

Hebrews 12:1 NLT

Three Starting Blocks

Conception

Foolishness that seems wise: the problem begins. "I was brought forth in iniquity, and in sin did my mother conceive me" (Ps. 51:5).

Conversion

A new way to live: the solution received. "Blessed are those whose lawless deeds are forgiven, and whose sins are covered; blessed is the man against whom the Lord will not count his sin" (Rom. 4:7–8).

Confession

A narrow road to travel: the battle engaged. "For the desires of the flesh are against the Spirit, and the desires of the Spirit are against the flesh, for these are opposed to each other, to keep you from doing the things you want to do" (Gal. 5:17).

The Severe Truth

Four or five times a year, I stand before thirty men and women to begin another seven-day School of Spiritual Direction. The same thought rattles me every time: if God really wants to make us a community of feminine women and masculine men, He has His work cut out for Him, work that will be all the more difficult if He plans for us to deeply connect with each other.

I know He is up to the job, but I also know that we must be willing for Him to do what needs doing. And what needs doing is nothing less than soul surgery, without anesthesia. It is a road difficult to traverse. This road leads us from *conception*, through *conversion*, and on into *confession*, until we reach the eternal *conclusion* of living fully alive in the dance of the forever-alive Trinity.

Ever since Eden, conception has created in us the opposite effect of what God desired in us. Every woman came into this world as a little girl *destined to open* and *determined to close*, wanting good relationships but wanting more to protect herself against bad relationships. And every man arrived on the scene as a little boy *destined to move* and *determined to stop*, eager to make a difference in other people's lives but more eager to never fail. We will neither understand nor appreciate what God must do unless we realize that each of us began our journey, our slow race to being fully alive, with a compelling desire to head in a disastrously wrong direction that we were convinced was right, or at least safe.

Here's what rattles me: if the way we think never changes, and if we never desire to head in the right direction, we have no chance to really live. On her own, no woman will wisely open herself to reveal the beauty of an inviting God, not when she smells danger. No woman will become feminine. And on his own, no man will sustain movement that reveals the beauty of a God who moves in love toward people who don't want Him, not if he anticipates little impact. No man will become masculine.

It is a severe truth with which we must reckon: *none of us will realize our God-appointed destiny as male or female unless deep repentance changes our minds and painful brokenness releases new desires.*

Old thinking, lies that we believe about what it means to be alive as men and women, is fixed in our minds with angry, threatened, and stubborn energy. And old desires, desires whose satisfaction we foolishly count on to help us feel alive, remain persuasively strong in our deceitful hearts.

But worse, our wrong thinking and foolish desires provide the world, the culture in which we live, with choice opportunities to shape how we relate to each other in a way that reflects the wisdom of hell. For all our growing up years, a disappointing and dangerous world has helped us come up with effective ways to protect ourselves from whatever might hurt us and to get from others whatever lets us feel good about ourselves. Personal comfort solidifies as our number-one priority.

Loving others more than we love ourselves may be accepted as a lofty virtue, but in real life it just doesn't make good sense to us. From conception, the first starting block, we are more committed to our individual well-being than to another's, and God's glory doesn't even appear on our radar screen. Girls find a way to close up and hide. Boys figure out how to move with minimum risk and maximum gain.

But everyone who sits with me as our School of Spiritual Direction begins is a Christian. Each of us has walked through the narrow gate of trusting Jesus to save us from the penalty of our sins and to give us the power to live a new way, to head in a different direction.

Somehow the Spirit moved and we came to our senses and realized how alone we were in our self-centeredness, how fully dead we were to God and to our design as human beings. Dressed in the filth of relational sin, we stood with heads bowed low in the presence of a relationally holy God, helplessly alone and hopelessly guilty.

And then we saw Jesus. We were converted. For the first time, we understood that He died to forgive us for our relationship-spoiling self-centeredness, for that inborn, proud spirit of entitlement that justified our demand to be treated well. And we believed that Jesus rose from the grave to pour His relational life into us, His Holy Spirit who gives us the power to desire relationship with God as our unchallenged highest good, and to pass on God's love to others at any cost to ourselves.

The Distorted Journey

At conversion, when we walked through the narrow gate, a new way to live opened before us. But more often than not, the idea of becoming feminine or masculine for God did not occur to us. The understanding of relational femininity and relational masculinity that glorifies God by revealing how He relates never entered my mind till nearly fifty years after my conversion.

In the life of each man and woman participating in the school a bad beginning (the first starting block) had given way to a new beginning, a good one (the second starting block). Conception directed us toward ourselves. Conversion aimed us in a much better direction: toward God first, then others.

But soon after conversion, it became clear that the narrow gate led us on to a narrow road, a rough path full of disappointment, discouragement, difficulties, and failure, an existence we could only define as tragic. Some Christians, however, were sufficiently "blessed" to be able to sustain a lifestyle of denial, to believe that the narrow road was narrow only in the sense of privileged membership, of an exclusive club of the elite who would be uniquely graced with good things like good kids, good money, and good health, and with healed emotions that would allow them to feel pretty good about themselves and their kids.

But that kind of denial can only be sustained by lowering our goals. The call to radical discipleship has to be reduced to an opportunity for pleasant Christianity if we're to keep believing the narrow road offers a comfortable journey. Following Jesus then means to care about others but to first make sure you're safe. See to it that life works well for you. Provide for others, but count on God to provide enough blessings for you to stay content. Be good to others and congratulate yourself on all that you do without ever exploring how others are impacted by you. Love everyone but cozy up only to those whose company you enjoy. Humble yourself but continue seeking the respect and admiration of others.

Post-conversion, after we're launched on our journey as Christians, most of us come up with some distorted understanding of the Christian life that allows us to believe that if we live well God will see to it that our lives go well. Nothing shatters that illusion quite so effectively as the realization of what it means to be fully alive as men and women for the glory of God. We prefer to keep on thinking that God's plan is for us to be fully alive in the enjoyment of pleasant circumstances, satisfying relationships, and happy feelings.

—

Midway through the seven-day School, we explore the Bible to see what it means to be a God-revealing feminine woman or a God-revealing masculine man. We look closely at how a spiritually forming woman opens herself to others to reveal the beauty of an indestructible gentle spirit and an undemanding quiet spirit, a way of relating that refuses to be controlled by fear. We discuss how a spiritually forming man moves toward others, pouring into others a life-giving love that is willing to endure indifference and criticism in order to draw others to the God who is always moving toward them.

The clearer our vision of relational femininity and masculinity becomes, the more clearly we see what needs to be given up to live fully alive for the glory of God as women and men. And then we realize, and welcome, how narrow the road must become to lead us to life. Life on the narrow road squeezes so much out of us that we thought we needed to live fully alive for God. A self-protective style of relating has to go. The self-affirming security of success can no longer be our goal. And the self-serving demand to be pursued and valued must be abandoned through repentance.

A vision of new life as feminine women and masculine men brings with it a call to a new kind of battle. No longer do we battle to have a good marriage. We now battle against everything inside us that gets in the way of living as wives or husbands, as women and men who are called to reveal God's beauty to our spouses.

No longer do we battle to have good kids. We now battle to be feminine moms and masculine dads. No longer do we battle to enjoy the good life of blessings. We pray for blessings and arrange for them insofar as we can. But something matters more. We enter the battle against the world, the flesh, and the devil in order to enjoy the better life of knowing God personally and revealing Him relationally.

When we battle to become whom we are destined to be as women and men, we discover the power of God to keep on fighting in any circumstance of life and in any felt condition of soul, to enjoy small victories and to persevere until finally we live fully alive in the presence of the God we strove to reveal in all our relationships.

To walk the narrow road to life, a third starting block is needed. *Conception* got us off on the wrong foot heading in the wrong direction, toward what promises life and delivers death. *Conversion* gave us a new beginning in a new relationship with Jesus that provided a new power to head in a new direction that delivers the life it promises.

But *confession* must follow conversion, as a way of life. Confession, as I'm using the term, means to never settle for the ease of an unexamined life. It means to look with brutal honesty at the reality of life in a fallen world as a converted but yet-to-be-glorified fallen woman or man, to see and reflect on all that's happening *around* us in our culture and in the world, all that's happening *between* us in our never fully successful efforts to build good relationships in loving community, and all that's happening *within* us where the only battle for which we're fully responsible is raging.

Confession sets us on the path to discover our Spirit-indwelt center, our core femininity or masculinity that is pressing to be released. I lead the School of Spiritual Direction, which is really the exercise of confession, with many convictions in mind, but none more immediately important than this one: God meets us where we are to empower us to move closer to where we long to be. He does not meet us where we pretend to be, or where we wish we were, or where in better days we once were. He meets us where we confess to be.

22

FROM CONCEPTION TO CONVERSION

Shaped Foolishness

The LORD saw that the wickedness of man was great in the earth, and that every intention of the thoughts of his heart was only evil continually. And the LORD regretted that he had made man on the earth, and it grieved him to his heart.

Genesis 6:5–6

And the earth was filled with violence. And God saw the earth, and behold, it was corrupt, for all flesh had corrupted their way on the earth.

Genesis 6:11–12

Folly [foolishness] is bound up in the heart of a child.

Proverbs 22:15

The creation itself will be set free from its bondage to corruption and obtain the freedom of the glory of the children of God. . . . And we know that for those who love God all things work together for good, for those who are called according to his purpose.

Romans 8:21, 28

The road to living life as it was meant to be lived is narrow. Jesus said so. But is it a bumpy, rugged, uphill climb, an arduous journey up a steep mountain? Or is it a smooth, level path that's narrow but, if walked with Jesus, a journey of joy? Perhaps it's a narrow descending road that takes us down into dark valleys where we must in faith depend on an unseen and unfelt Christ.

Or could it be all three, an uphill climb for a while, then a road down into frightening darkness, and then, as the prophet said, the "uneven ground" becomes level and the "rough places a plain" (Isa. 40:4). If I were to trust my experience, I'd say that the road to life is a lifelong cycle: up, down, level for a while, then up, down, and eventually level again.

What exactly is the road that leads women into femininity and men into masculinity? Let's think about that.

Realizations

You're a woman who is feeling convicted of how you're failing to be the relationally feminine woman you now understand God made you to be. As you've been reading this book, the Spirit has helped you to more clearly see how far short you fall of revealing God's relational glory by the way you relate to others, especially in your closest relationships. What now? What happens next? One woman said this to me:

> I know I feel unsafe. I've been hurt a lot. I keep my distance from anyone who makes me feel threatened, and I do it by coming across with a judgmental edge. I don't always hear the edge in my voice but I've been told it's there. I know I tend to be critical, but I really think I'm only critical of what ought to be criticized. I've always thought of myself as more honest than critical, a realist who doesn't wear rose-colored glasses. But now I'm realizing that I pick on faults in others that I don't think I have. So I feel superior, and helpful. I think I relate like that to feel good about myself, you know, able to say "Well, I'm not like so-and-so." I can see now how wrong that is, how unfeminine and unopen I am. And yet, I don't want to be open. I'm afraid nobody will like what's really inside, including me. But I don't know what to do. *How does change happen?*

My initial response to that woman was this: "You do feel bad about how you fail. You do want to change. And you've likely prayed for God to show you how to change. You're sincerely trying to bring the monster within you under your control. *But it's not working.*"

———

You're a man who is beginning to see that, by biblical definition, you're not a masculine man, at least not fully. You have no real friends, you angrily retreat from relationships you don't know how to handle, and you sometimes feel like a volcano of pressure waiting to explode. You're realizing that you move toward people more for your sake than theirs. And now you're wondering what to do about all that you're seeing about yourself. A friend said the following to me:

> I look together, but I don't feel together. When I slow down long enough to think, I feel afraid. I feel small, insignificant, obsessed with myself and how I'm coming across and how well my life is going. I can feel an arrogant, low-level anger always seething in me that sometimes just bursts out over little things in a huge rage. I've never thought so deeply about myself before. And I'd be really uncomfortable telling others what's going on in me. I don't like what I see. I'm not sure if I've ever been really close to anyone. Your picture of a bridge makes me realize I've never crossed it to connect deeply with people I claim to love. Sometimes I think I'd do anything, and I mean anything, to just feel strong and good and important, if even for just a moment. I'm not the man I want to be. But I'm a Christian. *And I have no idea how I'm supposed to really change.*

I listen to my friend and reply: "This is what I'm hearing. You're seeing, maybe for the first time, how poorly you relate. You know you're wrong but you have no clear idea what is so wrong in you that comes out in how wrongly you relate. You've meaningfully asked God to help you change. You've read a few good books on what it means to be a man. You're even in a men's group with guys who get pretty honest. *But whatever is wrong in you remains unidentified and still has real power to keep you relating poorly.*"

Like this woman and this man, if you're a Christian you've walked through the narrow gate. I became a Christian when I was eight years old. We're inside the gate. We've experienced genuine new birth, conversion to Christ, adoption into God's family, the never-to-be-removed indwelling of the Holy Spirit, an invitation to approach our divine Father just as we are to find help in time of need, and resurrection power that frees us to move toward others the way Jesus moved. Nothing's lacking. So what's wrong? What are we now to do? What's next?

The Root of David's Sin

It's time to follow Jesus on the narrow road. There is no other path that will form us into feminine women and masculine men. But what is it? What is the narrow road and how do we travel on it? King David's story has something to say about these questions.

Like each of us, he failed. Like very few of us, he knew why. And when he failed, he knew what to do. Perhaps David's worst violation of his gendered design came about when, after sending his soldiers off to war, he "stayed behind in Jerusalem" (2 Sam. 11:1 NLT). As commander in chief, he was called to move into battle, to always be about God's mission. But he took a break. He stopped.

Some might think that David deserved a break, that he was wisely exercising self-care. After all, he had already killed a bear and a giant and had led his mighty men and soldiers into many battles. But there are two kinds of self-care. The godly version stops moving in order to move again with renewed strength. David's version proved to be more of a retreat, not into renewing self-care but into depleting self-indulgence.

Within a day of his stopped movement, he committed adultery. While relaxing on the rooftop of his palace, he saw a woman whose physical beauty aroused lustful movement. A retreat like David's into ill-advised self-care, the kind that feels entitled to relief from the stress of moving rather than the kind that longs for a soul restored in order to keep moving, deepens a man's vulnerability to illegitimate pleasure.

Bathsheba got pregnant by David. When he found out, David arranged for further self-care, first through deceit and then through murder, both designed to preserve his reputation, not God's. Nothing gives the flesh more power than hiding its failure. David, a man after God's own heart (in Old Testament terms, he had entered through the narrow gate), had Bathsheba's husband, Uriah, killed. He then invited the widow to move in with him as his wife. It appeared that he got away with it. A new wife, a new child: things were going well.

"But the LORD was displeased with what David had done" (2 Sam. 11:27). Nathan, God's choice to provide David with spiritual direction, maneuvered the hiding sinner into open confession. Humbled by his failure more than angrily embarrassed over being caught, David simply said, "I have sinned."

But he added a telling phrase: "I have sinned *against the* LORD" (12:13, emphasis added). If I were Bathsheba's father or Uriah's brother, I might have had a reaction to David's choice of words. "You've sinned against my daughter! You've sinned against my brother!"

And of course David had done both. But David understood that moral failure, relational sin, was fueled by an evil energy lodged deep in his heart, a way of thinking that justified turning away from God when relief was more immediately and easily available elsewhere, pleasurable relief that David could arrange on his timetable.

David realized he was conceived in sin, that he was born a sinner, and that his passion to sin revealed itself in his choice to sin.

Christians today, myself included, tend to see the fruit of sin without recognizing its root. A theology of sin management encourages us to see little need to look deep in our hearts, to discover the energy of sin that was in us at conception and remains in us after conversion. The effect of such "broad road theology" is shallow repentance that fails to release the femininity or masculinity that lies deep in the soul of every image-bearer.

Shallow repentance looks something like this: we do something wrong and then we feel guilty. Feeling guilty also makes us feel bad, unhappy, irritable, and cold. We then dwell on our failure as a way of doing penance. Penance, of course, is pride. It's our way of telling God that He really ought to forgive us so we can feel better about ourselves. We weary God with tearful pledges to do better, promises we repeat after every failure. When we manage by serious self-effort to not commit our besetting sin for a season, we feel more proud than grateful, still self-absorbed. When we do fail again, whether in familiar or new ways, bad feelings start the same cycle of shallow repentance all over again.

David took a different route. He reflected on the monster within, the anti-God virus that made sinful behavior attractive and seemingly justified, even necessary. "For I was born a sinner—yes, from the moment my mother conceived me" (Ps. 51:5 NLT). In the next verse, the word translated *inward being* or *secret heart* in most of our Bibles literally means the hidden regions of the soul where secrets are kept, where we keep whatever we don't want to see out of sight. David prayed that God would teach him wisdom from "even there" (v. 6 NLT).

Walking the narrow road requires deep repentance. And repentance becomes deep when we learn *wisdom from the womb*: from conception bad things have been going on inside us that will plague us for as long as we're alive in this world.

Wisdom from the Womb

Lesson 1

From conception to conversion, boys and girls have no greater desire than to arrange for their own well-being through resources they can control. Their greatest desire is their greatest problem.

Little girls, as I earlier mentioned, begin life *destined to open* and *determined to close*. Little boys emerge from the womb *destined to move* and *determined to stop*. Question: What was going on during the nine months from conception to birth that got all of us off to such a bad start? Girls are wired to open to reveal Jesus but they invariably close to protect themselves. Boys are designed to move to reveal Jesus but they inevitably stop to avoid failure. Why?

From the moment of conception, while arms and legs and eyes and lungs are forming, a *capacity to relate* is forming as well, a capacity to connect with God and others as male or female. But, as David understood, at the same time a *passion for self* is growing, an energy with no higher goal than feeling good, a desire that aims our capacity to relate *away* from relating to God on His terms and *toward* self-management, toward a self-produced experience of personal fulfillment and safety.

In simpler terms, you and I began our existence assuming that "It's all about me."

During life before birth, the child is safely and comfortably dependent. The mother's womb takes care of every felt need. Then birth happens. When the child enters the open, disconnected space of this world, complacent dependency instantly becomes terrified dependency. *Is anyone there? What just happened? Someone, please, be* with *me! Be there, be here,* for *me!*

Good parents reply, "I am here. I am with you. I am for you. I know what you need and I will supply what you need. I will never leave you or forsake you. You are safe. You are wanted. You are loved." Good parents give their newborn child his or her first taste of Jesus.

But the stage is set for disappointment. No parent is capable of responding to a child's terror with dependable sensitivity or discerning wisdom, not perfectly. Parental failure, which is inevitable, kicks into action a child's foolishness, which is inborn. The God-like capacity for relationship is soon experienced as a God-dependent need for relationship in a child who foolishly does not seek after God. "No one understands; no one seeks for God" (Rom. 3:11).

Movement away from God, the definition of foolishness, reveals a passion for self, a determination to find satisfaction in whatever the self can manage. And that foolish passion has been "bound up" in a child's inward parts since conception (see Prov. 22:15).

The helpless cry of an infant becomes the entitled demand of a toddler that continues to rule in every male and female until conversion. "Please be with me. I need you!" morphs into "Be there for me. I insist!" Terrified girls (and women) designed to *invite* others to enjoy the beauty of an inviting God now *require* others to meet their needs: "Enjoy *me*! Delight yourself in *me*! Pursue *me*! If you don't, I will close my heart to you and open whatever I can find in me that will get others to want me."

Terrified boys (and men), shaped by God to find their significance by impacting others with the God-revealing movement of love, demand something for themselves: "Respect *me*! Notice *me*! Affirm that what I offer makes a positive difference in your life. If you don't, I'll stop moving toward you and I'll move toward others with whatever I have that will get what I need."

Wisdom from the womb puts us in touch with a problem that began at conception, developed in childhood, and is still with us today, opposing every prompting of God's Spirit. This wisdom leads to deep repentance.

Lesson 2

With no stronger desire within us than to feel alive without turning to God, our life experiences have the power to shape our passion for self, to teach us how we can relate in ways that will avoid what we fear and gain what we want. A self-serving relational style develops in all of us.

At his cunning best, Satan works through life's experiences, both relational and circumstantial, to suggest ways for us to arrange for what
we feel we need, ways that will seem moral, perhaps even "Christian."
Our foolishness embraces the world's wisdom and our flesh is socialized,
dressed up to look good—and if not good, at least necessary. We have a
right to live as we choose, to relate in any way that feels right to us, or so
we stubbornly think.

Little girls foolishly close their hearts and display their will. The feeling
of power feels good, especially to a girl whose father abused or abandoned
her. Power over food leads to anorexia. Power over others opens the door
to sensuality and promiscuity, to displayed competence and drivenness, to
justified retreat from painful relationships, to winning approval through
compulsive kindness.

Little boys foolishly give up on relating well and move toward success.
The feeling of significance that achievement provides feels good, especially
to a boy whose mother was controlling or whose dad was critical. Movement toward success leads to dreams of athletic prowess, of recognized
leadership in business or church or politics, of easy pleasure through pornography or adultery or possessions.

Wisdom from the womb exposes the foolishness that directs so much
of how we live and even the apparently good choices we make. Deep repentance follows deep brokenness over relational failure.

Lesson 3

Deep repentance requires deep conviction that emerges in deep brokenness. Until we realize that without God we can do nothing but sin, we will
never understand the futility of self-effort, the delights of God-dependence,
and the power of pride-driven flesh. And we will remain unfeminine women
and unmasculine men.

Through Jeremiah, God severely scolded the religious leaders of Israel
for providing "superficial treatments for my people's mortal wound" (Jer.
6:14 NLT). When my doctor told me I had cancer, I thanked him. I needed
to realize that I had a physical "mortal wound" that diet and exercise
wouldn't cure.

A close friend once told me that he no longer wanted to share his real
struggles with me. Stunned, I asked why. His answer stunned me even more:

"Larry, when I tell you my problems I feel like I become your project, your opportunity to display your gifts in order to feel good about yourself."

A new depth of repentance followed, though not immediately. I bristled for a while. But then I followed the Spirit as He led me to search my heart. From a grade-school kid who won the spelling bee to a graduate student who drove himself to excel, I realized I was compensating for undeveloped social skills and covering my fear of relational failure by performing well in the academic world; I became Dr. Crabb and lost Larry. My battle to "live Larry" continues.

A passion for self had been lodged in my inward parts before I even emerged from my mother's womb. That passion was then shaped into a way of relating that served my fear-driven demand to "be someone." My friend's rebuke helped me realize that, without God, I could do nothing but sin. And it became a little clearer that I had no power to manage my sin. I could only confess it.

With God, I am slowly learning that God's grace means I can come to Him with an empty soul I cannot fill and a broken way of relating I cannot change. When I do, a strange filling happens and I feel a *desire* to relate as a man, whether others call me Dr. Crabb, or Larry, or husband, or Dad, or Pop-Pop. And brokenness over relational failure yields an awareness of a new *power* within me. I participate in the divine nature, the same nature that was released in Jesus when He lived and died in this world, the nature that is revealed in me and released from me only in brokenness.

Self-obsessed men and women foolishly demand from others what only God can give, what God longs to give. We then realize, as God's Spirit works in us, that our way of relating leaves us empty and is unspeakably ugly. If we then confess ourselves to be hopeless and helpless in the presence of a holy and merciful God, we begin our walk on the narrow road that will free us to live as feminine women and masculine men.

The problem that keeps us from becoming who we long to be is deep. God's solution is deeper. It's to that solution that we now turn.

23

NEW LIFE

The central Christian belief is that Christ's death has somehow put us right with God and given us a fresh start.

Fallen man is not simply an imperfect creature who needs improvement: he is a rebel who must lay down his arms. . . . [This] is what Christians call repentance. Now repentance is no fun at all. . . . It means unlearning all the self-conceit and self-will that we have been training ourselves into.

The main thing we learn from a serious attempt to practice the Christian virtues is that we fail.

The only help I [Christ] will give is to help you become perfect. You may want something less: but I will give you nothing less.

[Christ] came into this world and became man in order to spread to other men [and women] the kind of life He has—by what I call "good infection."

C. S. Lewis[1]

Conception gets all of us off to a very bad start. Little boys and little girls begin life loving only themselves. Even then, and from when they were only

1. C. S. Lewis, *Mere Christianity* (New York: MacMillan, 1943), 57, 55, 125, 171, and 153, respectively.

a thought in His mind, God loves them. And should one of them die before willfully rejecting Jesus, God welcomes that child to live forever in heaven with Him. But they do begin life with a serious problem. *We* do, all of us.

Until conversion, no woman is on her way to becoming biblically feminine and no man is growing into biblical masculinity. A feminine woman loves by resting in God's love and living to reveal to others the inviting love of Jesus. A masculine man loves by counting on God's love and living for no higher purpose than revealing to others the movement of God's love. But no one who is dead to God loves like God. And until conversion, no one is alive to God.

Love Is Life

It is a severe and frightening truth, but a truth filled with hope: without the Holy Spirit pouring supernatural power into a forgiven, broken, and repentant heart, no man or woman loves anyone in a way that reveals the relational character of God. But with the Holy Spirit's empowerment, there is new life to live and a new way to live it.

Paul agrees. Writing to Christians, to converted sinners, he reminds them of what was true before their conversion.

> And you *were* dead [not now] in the trespasses and sins in which you *once* walked [no longer], following the course of this world, following the prince of the power of the air, the spirit that is now at work in the sons of disobedience—among whom we all once lived in the passions of our flesh, carrying out the desires of the body and the mind, and were by nature children of wrath [in another translation, *subject to God's anger*], like the rest of mankind. (Eph. 2:1–3, emphasis added)

Without Christ, none of us loves the way we were designed to love. We relate to meet our needs, not to reveal God's love. Of course we're subject to God's anger. What else can a holy God of love do but hate whatever spoils the joy and ruins the relationships of people He loves, whatever gets in the way of His people valuing Him as their supreme good and revealing Him to others as their highest purpose?

Small wonder Dostoyevsky described hell as the suffering of being unable to love. That suffering ends in Christ. "But God is so rich in mercy, and he loved us so much, that even though we were dead because of our sins, *he gave us life*" (v. 4 NLT, emphasis added). It's God's life that makes us able to love.

Only conversion to Christ provides the life that enables us to love like Christ. John, the apostle who several times referred to himself as "the one whom Jesus loved," told us that we can "know that we have passed out of death into life, because we love the brothers. Whoever does not love abides in death" (1 John 3:14). Christians love other Christians, and together they love the world by revealing God's love for sinful people. At least that's the plan. Converted people no longer need experience the suffering of being unable to love but can now know the freedom and delight of being able to love.

In his Gospel, the same apostle recorded these words he had heard from Jesus: "A new commandment I give to you, that you love one another: just as I have loved you, you also are to love one another. By this all people will know that you are my disciples, if you have love for one another" (John 13:34–35).

Add these truths together and you come up with good news: a Christian woman can now open herself to invite godly movement from everyone, from people who love her or hate her. She can become a feminine woman. A Christian man can now move toward others with the love of Jesus, toward people who respect him or dismiss him. He can become a masculine man.

Conversion brings new life to the converted, but it also brings with it a new battle. Before conversion, a man's or woman's battle to live well as a responsible, caring, and good person was fought between unsocialized self-centeredness and socialized self-centeredness. From conception to conversion, whether conversion happens at age eight or eighty, our most virtuous deeds were, in God's eyes "like a polluted garment" (Isa. 64:6). Until we came alive in Christ, the best we could do was put pretty clothes on a rotting corpse and cover the stench of decay with perfume.

But no longer, not after conversion. The corpse is alive. Easter morning has dawned. A new heart within a new creation is beating in the rhythm of new life. The relational life of the Trinity is now alive in us, prompting and enabling every Christian man and woman to relate either with masculine or feminine power that reveals the invisible God to a blind world. The glory the Father gave Jesus, the opportunity to reveal divine love through human relating, has now been given to us. It is a miracle of unimaginable proportions.

But the fruit of the miracle ripens slowly. And the miracle, wonderful though it is, begins a new struggle. The converted fight a new battle whose complete victory will not be won till heaven. A converted woman wants to reveal God's invitational life through her style of relating, but still she feels a compelling urge to protect herself, to close herself to others when she senses danger, sometimes by controlling others, other times by retreating from others behind a thick skin of shyness, competence, revenge, or coldness.

A converted man feels similarly conflicted. He battles against a powerful tendency to resist the call to move toward others with costly love and to stop moving toward anyone (especially a wife) who might not respond with the warmly affirming recognition he so badly wants. That same tendency encourages him to move toward success he can manage, toward relationships that require little personal courage, toward pleasures that can be enjoyed without risking relational movement.

The battle between the self-centered flesh and the God-centered spirit is on. How does God's Spirit lead us to fight the battle? By trying harder? Through programs, recipes, and formulas to follow? By exploring our inner world? Through identifying the forces hidden deep in our psyches that line up against each other? By practicing spiritual disciplines? By engaging in prescribed activities that stir an experience of God's presence and release His power in our souls?

Of course. Trying harder, developing insight, and practicing disciplines all have value. But Jesus told us that we will find the life we're after only if we walk through this world on a narrow road. What did He mean? Is it possible that, with the best of intentions, many of us are traveling on a broad road and only thinking we're on the narrow one that Jesus talked about? Does the narrow road require more of us than effort, insight, and discipline?

Foolishness dies hard. The courage of wisdom grows slowly. The forces of foolishness are strong: *self-centeredness*, an attitude that so easily assumes "it's all about me"; *proud independence*, an insistence on having control over whatever means most to me; and a *demanding spirit*, an angry sense of entitlement to fair treatment from others and to feeling good about

myself and my life. These enemy soldiers present themselves as allies to
our well-being as they wage war against the converted heart.

The battle to let wisdom rule, to relate as Spirit-controlled open women
and moving men, requires more of us than effort, insight, and discipline.

The woman that every man wants to avoid is described in Proverbs 21:9
as *quarrelsome*. The Hebrew word could be translated *referee*, the person
on the basketball court with a whistle. Whistle-blowing women, women
who believe it's their job to point out where others, especially husbands,
are wrong so that the game is played according to their rules, will only
drop their whistles on the narrow road.

The man that frustrates every woman is too cowardly to move toward
others like the God who hears, listens, remembers, and moves. Relationally
frozen men, weak men who selfishly keep their distance from commitment
that risks exposure of the strength they lack, will feel the thawing power
of God's Spirit, a power that releases courage, only on the narrow road.

Perhaps, like me, you really do want to walk the narrow road to the
relational life you were designed and redeemed for. But, also like me, you
will likely discover that the journey initially leads us most often onto a
still-broad road that narrows only after two legs of the journey fail to form
us into the men and women we were designed to become.

Call these two legs Phase 1 and Phase 2.

Phase 1: Aiming for the "Blessed Life"—Get It Right So Life Goes Well

Jesus made it clear: *the way to life is knowing God* (see John 17:3). Knowing God well enough to want nothing more than to relate like God, in any
circumstance of life or condition of soul, defines the good life. It's what it
means to be fully alive as men and women for God.

But we still think that a satisfying relationship *with* a spouse is to be
valued more than relating well *to* a spouse, even to a disagreeable spouse.
Parenting with a power that produces well-behaved children seems more
important to us than parenting with a power that reveals God to our children, whether they turn out well or not.

A full bank account can mean more to us than the fullness of God's
Spirit. We're often more interested in a healthy body than a healthy soul.

Tell me I have cancer and I'll schedule surgery while I pray. Tell me I'm self-centered and I'll schedule a tee time as I smile.

We pursue what we most value. If I value a blessed life over a God-revealing way of relating, if I desire legitimately good things that, in my immaturity, bring me more happiness than they bring me the power to love well in a difficult life, I will negotiate with God and think it's worship. I will pray, go to church, and read my Bible to better understand what He wants me to do in order to persuade Him to give me the blessings I want.

In our search for the narrow road, many Christians find our way onto a broad road that we think is the good narrow one because it promises to deliver the blessings we assume God most wants to provide. We aim no higher than the "blessed life." And when life goes well, we "worship" God for cooperating with our agenda. "Get it right so life goes well"—a broad road most of us travel on our way to the narrow road.

A sincere Christian woman longs to live well, to follow Jesus. Perhaps without realizing it, her real motive is to feel loved by her husband or to attract a man to marry her. She reads Christian books on mothering hoping to be respected by her children as they follow her lead. Perhaps her resolve to live well is energized by the desire to be valued in her work or to remain healthy and to feel attractive. She is a rule-keeper, trying hard to get it right so life goes well. She values the "blessed life" over the *better life* of knowing God well and revealing Him to others. In the process, she is grieving the Spirit.

She is also quenching the Spirit—who is providing unused power not for her to live well so life goes well, but to love well, to experience God's presence in her soul through expressing God's character by how she relates. She is living in the power of the flesh, living more for the blessings of life that she can enjoy than for the privilege of living a life that God can enjoy.

Suppose a Christian man aims for nothing greater than the satisfaction available in a good marriage, good children, career success, decent health, and a good reputation among colleagues and friends. The man is walking a broad road, aiming for the "blessed life," living a life that doesn't require the Spirit's power. He is an idolater, worshiping good things from God more than God Himself.

Neither this woman nor this man is yet walking the narrow road that surfaces their deep longing to reveal God by the way they relate. When we recognize no greater good than the "blessed life," our obedience becomes manipulation, our prayers negotiation.

With hard-to-appreciate mercy, God may answer none of these prayers. Blessings may be withdrawn. Blessings that once seemed satisfying may now feel empty. God will do what is necessary to aim us toward a greater good than the "blessed life." Eventually, we find ourselves no longer living for withdrawn or unsatisfying blessings but now for relief, relief from the pain of emptiness. It is then that Phase 2 begins, a slightly narrower road. We now aim for the "healed life."

Phase 2: Aiming for the "Healed Life"—Numb the Pain to Feel Better

Two kidney stones have made it clear to me that severe pain demands immediate relief. In the middle of physical pain, drugs become my dearest friends—not prayer, drugs. Relational pain has a similar effect. The earth trembles when "a bitter woman . . . finally gets a husband" (Prov. 30:23 NLT). She demands that her man relieve the pain in her heart.

"A slave who becomes a king" will also cause a relational earthquake (see vv. 21–22 NLT). A man who has long felt himself to be a failure, inadequate and insignificant, will use others however he can to help him to feel better about himself.

Relational pain that seems to justify a demand for relief leaves our *souls* in pain. No one treats us exactly as we desire. Nothing happens exactly as we want. We feel alone, unseen and unheard, disconnected. Recreational drugs help. Pornography works. Hard work and busyness numb the nagging discomfort in our souls.

Perhaps we seek God, not to relate well despite our pain but for relief, for healing from the painful wounds of life. Soul pain generates a desire for nothing more than a soothing experience of God. It's difficult to believe that a loving God would ask us to reveal a God we don't first experience, to love someone else when we feel empty. One man put it to me this way: "Until I feel good about myself, I can't really be there for anyone else."

But that attitude fuels narcissism and a lifelong search for a fully satisfying experience of *self* provided by God's felt presence. In too many circles, the gospel of experiencing God's healing presence has replaced the gospel of revealing God's relational nature. When we give up trying hard to get it right so that life goes well, aiming for the "blessed life," we take up the search for relief so that we feel better. We aim for the "healed life."

When we feel good, whether through lively worship, spiritual disciplines, ministry busyness, or prayer-centered counseling, we assume we've been "healed by God." But if we remain unaware of how far short of loving like Jesus we continue to fall, our healing is suspect. Jeremiah berated spiritual leaders who offered superficial healing for mortal wounds, healing that left those who were healed still unashamed of "their disgusting actions" (see Jer. 6:13–15). Peter told us that Christ's wounds healed us, not of our relational or soul pain, but of our relational failure, of "straying like sheep" from the Shepherd of our souls (see 1 Pet. 2:24–25). The healing that Christ gives empowers us to relate well, not to always feel good.

Women who report healing from God without becoming better able to reveal the invitational nature of God's love have not advanced in relational femininity. They may be happy, but they are not feminine.

Men who claim to be healed of feeling empty and insignificant without valuing even more their opportunity to reveal the moving nature of God's love have not grown in relational masculinity. They may feel confident and alive, but they are not masculine.

We aim for the "blessed life" and come away proud or discouraged. Our efforts to live right either work or don't work. If they don't work (and that can be a blessing), if we feel the pain of disappointment and defeat, or of futility and boredom, we then aim for the "healed life." After a while, the search for relief leaves us either superficially healed or deeply troubled.

Conception leads us off in a wrong direction. *Conversion* makes us alive to God, able to love, wanting to love, and aware of the call to know God and reveal Him by how we relate. But conversion brings with it a new battle. When the battle wearies us, first from our efforts to arrange for blessings and then from our search for relief from pain, we are ready to face a reality that will lead us onto the true narrow road, the only road that moves us toward our destiny to live as feminine women and masculine men. It's time to continue the journey from the third starting block: *confession*.

24

LIFE EMERGES

When the Road Narrows

No possible degree of holiness or heroism which has ever been recorded of the greatest saints is beyond what He is determined to produce in every one of us in the end. The job will not be completed in this life: but He means to get us as far as possible before death. That is why we must not be surprised if we are in for a rough time.

C. S. Lewis[1]

In every Christian there is both "flesh" and "spirit." . . . So in every Christian there is a war, the flesh seeking to rule and dominate the spirit, and the spirit seeking to subdue the flesh.

John Owen[2]

Letting your sinful nature control your mind leads to death. But letting the Spirit control your mind leads to life and peace.

Romans 8:6 NLT

1. C. S. Lewis, *Mere Christianity* (New York: MacMillan, 1943), 173–74.
2. John Owen, *Spiritual Mindedness*, abridged by R. J. K. Law (Carlisle, PA: The Banner of Truth Trust, 2009), 1.

I would redeem them, but they speak lies against me. They do not cry to me from the heart, but they wail upon their beds.

Hosea 7:13–14

Sue, a Christian woman, had been living in self-protective fear for more than forty years, beginning after a neighbor severely abused her when she was four. Soon after, her father saw her sitting by herself crying. He was not a gentle man. Sue remembers her dad impatiently asking, "What's the matter with you?"

Decades later, as she was telling me the story, she could clearly see herself in that moment as a terrified little girl huddled on the couch with her legs pulled up to her chest and her face buried against her knees.

"When Daddy so gruffly asked me why I was crying, a wave of fear swallowed me. I felt paralyzed. All I could say when I looked up into his face was, 'Nothing's wrong. I'm okay.' He looked puzzled in a disgusted sort of way, said 'Well, stop crying then,' and walked away. I think I've been a closed woman ever since, scared to death to open any part of me to anyone, terrified they wouldn't see me. I'd be invisible."

As we talked, the road on which she was walking narrowed. We thought together about the terror controlling her and how that traumatic event, among several others, had shaped her way of relating with family, friends, and a particularly difficult supervisor at work whose curt manner reminded her of her father. Sue became acutely aware of two things: an empty space within her soul that was loudly screaming for a love she had never experienced and a jaw-clenched determination to always play it safe and never emerge from behind a self-protective wall that made it impossible for anyone to hurt her so severely again.

From conception, Sue's natural inclination, like all of ours, was to look after herself. From her conversion at age twenty, she had been aware of a deep and genuine desire to live for God. As we talked, I sensed it was the Holy Spirit's time for Sue to now continue her journey from Starting Block 3: confession. Deep places within her were becoming unsettled. Long-denied realities were hitting her with previously unfelt power.

With strong but still not easily expressed emotion, she confessed how desperately alone she felt: unseen, unheard, and unknown. But then, strangely enough, a sober calmness came over her as she understood how self-righteously and stubbornly justified she felt in relating to others as a fearfully victimized and a protectively, vengefully closed woman. Self-centered resolve was alive beneath her self-threatening terror. She saw it. The Spirit of Holy Love was at work. God seized the opportunity of both the hopeless emptiness she was now experiencing and the helpless broken-ness she was now confessing over her unholy way of relating that advanced no purpose beyond her own. His Spirit performed a miracle.

Her painfully felt emptiness became a thirsty longing for the God whose love she passionately wanted to know. And brokenness over her lifelong relational failure opened her ears to hear the gentle voice of her heavenly Father whispering, *I love you as you are. I have always loved you. I see you. I know you. You are forgiven. I will hold you as you cry.* The memory of her harsh father returned, but now, as a four-year-old girl grown into an adult woman, she reported, "a sparkling light of delight penetrated my heart."

Not long after, she was called into a meeting with her difficult supervisor. I then received this letter:

> The night before, as the realization came that I would be facing him the next day, I found myself moving into self-protection. Also, I recognized a certain disdain and grumbling spirit toward him. As I took these to God, soon He was convicting me of the sin in my heart, and He showed me it was part of my determination to maintain a self-protective wall. As long as I blame my supervisor for all my troubles, I can justify myself and justify remaining closed by not speaking up.
>
> That was not fun to see. But I knew it was true. I confessed this to God and opened myself to what He wanted me to do, who He wanted me to be, as a woman. It was then I became surprisingly aware of Him, of His delight and of Sue being alive. I could love. I *wanted* to love. What joy and inner, quiet beauty and strength I felt.
>
> As I walked into the meeting yesterday, I walked in free and alive, not self-protected! I walked in very aware of my center as an opened feminine woman. I related to him as God directed and didn't feel intimidated. Yesterday was a great beginning of a new woman. The paralysis I felt when my father asked me why I was crying was gone. It could no longer control me. Wow! I wanted to dance! Actually, I found myself dancing out of delight and freedom. I was worshiping God with my whole being.

The life of God emerged in Sue when the road she was walking narrowed. Her narrow road stretched ahead, toward wide places of life.

Ted, a Christian man, came across to others as a walking apology. His style of relating begged others to feel sorry for him, to hold him responsible for nothing, to accept his excuses for how badly he so often failed. Ted was in a position of spiritual leadership, seminary trained and blessed with a good mind. But his ministry was not going well. People under him were regularly complaining to people over him. He felt discouraged and defeated, worthy only of the pity he felt he deserved.

I asked Ted about his family. He weakly replied, "I don't know why my wife puts up with me. Sometimes she gets pretty frustrated and tells me she wishes I stood up for myself."

"What do you say when she tells you that?"

"I tell her I'm sorry. Maybe I feel a little irritated. I wish she understood how bad I feel about myself. I usually shrug my shoulders and walk away. I don't know what else to do."

Ted was not moving as a man. I prayed that he would feel the road narrowing.

His oldest son, living in another state pursuing a graduate degree, had just gotten his girlfriend pregnant. He had told his parents about his dilemma a week before my conversation with Ted—providential timing.

"What did you do when you heard the news?"

"Well, I wasn't home when he called. My wife told me about it that evening. She was crying."

"What did you do?"

"I didn't know what to do, so I prayed with her and told her we'd get through it somehow. I guess I should have called my son, but I wasn't sure he'd want to hear from me."

"This happened a week ago?"

"Yes."

"And you haven't contacted him since?"

"No."

As a young husband and father, Ted had been aiming for the "blessed life." For years, he had done what he could, what he thought God wanted him to do, and he was depending on God to see to it that his life would go well. When his marriage ran into conflict, when his son's sexual fun shamed his family, and when his ministry took an extra-deep nosedive, Ted felt overwhelmed, angrily self-pitying, and thoroughly inadequate.

In our conversation, he assured me that he prayed, he wept, he read his Bible. Nothing helped. With the "blessed life" out of reach, Ted was longing to experience the "healed life." It didn't come.

A reality soon hit Ted, an old truth that was new to him. During several more conversations we explored his background long enough for him to see that his father, a pastor, had been emotionally absent from his family, and likely as a reaction, his mother had become dutifully efficient in her mothering, not warmly engaged. When I asked him what "life message" he had received from his parents, he trembled, thought for moment, and then fighting back tears, said, "That there's not much to me."

Further conversations about his current relationships with his wife, son, and subordinates and supervisors in ministry opened his eyes to meaningfully see and own that his way of relating was inexcusably weak. He felt empty, devoid of whatever strength was needed to move with non-defensive love into his wife's heart, to move with a mentor's wisdom into his son's dilemma, and to move with humble courage into his supervisor's criticism of his ministry. He left our time together feeling more defeated and helpless than before. His road to life was narrowing.

Two days later, we chatted again. I sensed an unfamiliar confidence in his words:

> I've never felt worse than after our last conversation. I realized I had managed to see myself as more mistreated than weak. But when I admitted to myself how weakly I was relating to just about everybody, I wanted to do the world a favor and curl up in a corner somewhere and hide there for the rest of my life.
>
> But something happened last night. I couldn't sleep. Something was nagging at me. I'm pretty sure now it was the Holy Spirit. Almost suddenly at about two in the morning, I saw how wrong I was to be so weak. I was failing my wife, my son, and the people I was supposed to be spiritually leading. This may be an overstatement, but maybe not: *I think it was the first time I really saw myself as a sinner.* I left our last conversation feeling embarrassed and humiliated and, to be honest, pretty ticked at you for showing me how weak I was.
>
> But I come into this conversation now feeling troubled, more humbled than humiliated; and convicted, not embarrassed. How I'm living is wrong; it isn't revealing anything about God to anyone. I still feel empty, but now I feel broken too. I'm not sure I can explain it, but I'm aware of a new kind of hope I've never felt before. I feel strong, that I can move toward others with a new kind of strength.

True to form, God's Spirit was seizing the opportunity He had created when He opened Ted's eyes to see and embrace his emptiness without trying to fill it, and to see and be broken by his relational failure without promising to fix it.

Two weeks later, I received a letter from Ted.

> I sat yesterday with a committee from my denomination that provides oversight for my ministry. They raked me over the coals more severely than I could have anticipated. *And I didn't crumble!* I owned my failure, but not as a defeated wimp, and I didn't beg for a second chance to do better. I challenged their perspectives when I saw things differently and I told them that whether I remained in this ministry position or moved on to something else, I was confident that God was releasing me to move with more spiritual power than before. When I told my wife what happened in that meeting, she smiled and asked, "What happened to you? I like it!" I have yet to move toward my son, but I'm looking forward to the privilege. It feels less like a burden I can't handle and more like an opportunity to reveal something about God to him.

Spiritual growth into relational masculinity or femininity does not always restore the "blessed life" or usher in the "healed life." Our lives may remain unblessed by pleasant circumstances and unhealed from painful emotions. Two weeks later, the supervisory committee called for a second meeting with Ted to inform him that his responsibilities and income were being reduced, and that he was now on three months' probation. Ted immediately felt a tidal wave of inadequacy, frustration, anger, and terror sweep over him as his already narrow road narrowed even more.

As I write these words, Ted is still reeling and trusting, embracing his weakness and owning his failure. With the apostle Paul, he is groaning inwardly and waiting eagerly, supported by a small community of friends who believe in Ted and in the work God is accomplishing in him and plans to accomplish through him.

The Abundant Life

God often uses present troubles to nourish an eternal perspective. "For I consider that the sufferings of this present time are not worth comparing with the glory that is to be revealed to us" (Rom. 8:18). Ted is no longer demanding either the "blessed life" of things going well in this world or the "healed life" of always feeling the presence of God. The *abundant life* of revealing God to others in any circumstance of life or condition of soul is alive within him, and it is slowly emerging as his road continues to narrow.

I share these stories of Sue and Ted because they are typical of what happens when the few whom Jesus spoke of who find the narrow road walk on it throughout life—and stay on it long enough to discover what it means to be relationally alive as feminine women and masculine men.

As we now consider the "rough times" that C. S. Lewis told us to anticipate when we follow Jesus, keep clearly in mind a vision of what God is dong in us and wants to do through us as the narrow road He leads us on narrows. The rough times involve the war between the flesh and spirit that goes on in every one of us who is converted, the war that continues to rage within us till we die. As the narrowness of the road to life squeezes out of us our dependence on blessings or healing for joy, we will better understand what the prophet Hosea meant when he said that as we walk the narrow road we must "cry from the heart" and not "wail from our beds," even though wailing, demanding blessings and relief, comes more naturally and feels justified (see Hos. 7:14). No one who remains committed to the "blessed life" or, when dreams shatter, demands to experience the "healed life," will be drawn to the abundant life that Jesus tells us will come to all who walk the narrow road, "who cry from their hearts" as they repent of feeling entitled to any good thing.

Remember what happened two thousand years ago when Jesus provided, as He often does today, a taste of the "blessed life." Five thousand hungry people enjoyed a good lunch as Jesus multiplied five loaves of bread and two fish to feed them all, with second helpings available. They were excited. "This is indeed the Prophet who is to come into the world" (John 6:14), they declared, thinking Jesus was the prophet Moses had promised would come to make everything right (see Deut. 18:15, 18).

The crowd was so impressed with what they now realized Jesus could do for them that, like many disciples today, they wanted to make Him king. But "Jesus withdrew" (John 6:15). Why? He will only give us what He knows we need, not what we think we need. The people, however, persisted. When they found Him again the next day and were eager for more of the "blessed life," Jesus made it clear that His plan did not center on providing food to fill their stomachs, but food that would make them alive to God.

He went on to speak about "the bread of God," the true bread that came down from heaven from the Father (see vv. 32–33). The people, still hungry for material blessings but now made curious by the prophet's words, said, "Sir, give us this bread always." Jesus then explained that the bread He was offering was relationship with Him, bread that would make them alive to God and able to relate like God.

Imagine not having eaten for a week and seeing a sign that reads, "Available Inside: Better Food Than You've Ever Enjoyed." You walk in, sit at a table prepared with linen cloth, silverware, fine china, a wine goblet, and a crystal water glass. A man, obviously the owner of the restaurant, approaches your table and, rather then handing you a leather-bound menu describing mouth-watering entrees, he sits down next to you, smiles, and says, "Let's get to know each other. You're hungrier for a friend than for a meal. I want to be that friend, the best friend you've ever had. Let me be your food."

You likely would respond to that man much like His first-century disciples responded to Jesus: "You supplied lunch. How about dinner tonight and breakfast tomorrow morning? You want us to eat and drink You? What on earth are You talking about?" I suspect they were thinking similar thoughts when they said among themselves and to Jesus: "This is a hard saying: who can listen to it" (v. 60).

In typical fashion, Jesus went on to deepen their confusion. "It is the Spirit who gives life; the flesh is no help at all. The words that I have spoken to you are spirit and life" (v. 63).

"But Lord," we say, "I want a meal of real food, food that I can chew and swallow, that tastes good and keeps me healthy. I want blessings now so that I can enjoy my life and healing that lets me enjoy myself."

Jesus patiently replies that He offers soul food (literally) that will let us live whether we starve to death or not, whether our marriage is terrible, or our children break our hearts, or a close friend betrays us, or we lose our jobs, or our health badly fails; food that will keep us relating with other-centered love when we feel discouraged and empty, defeated and disconsolate; food that we can continue to enjoy when we stumble and fall, perhaps then even enjoy more than ever.

"Jesus, wouldn't it make more sense for You to *prevent* all that suffering, to skip the rough times and provide a blessed life of comfort and prosperity and a healed life of self-esteem and self-confidence?" Apparently, most of His followers were asking that same question. I know I sometimes do. But Jesus wouldn't budge. He knew He was offering something far better than what they wanted, what I sometimes still want.

When the Road Has Narrowed

His plans, however, made no sense to them. His ways were too far above them for their minds to appreciate. So, "many of his disciples turned back and no longer walked with him" (v. 66). If He won't provide the "blessed life" and the "healed life," we'll look for a more cooperative Messiah. And scores of Jesus-followers today, with the help of their spiritual leaders, are turning back, leaving the narrow road and imagining a Jesus who better suits their preferences, a Jesus who promises the blessed life of personal comfort and the healed life of self-love.

It was then that Jesus turned to the Twelve and asked, "Do you want to go away as well?" (v. 67). Peter, always the group spokesman, replied, "Lord, to whom shall we go? You have the words of eternal life, and we have believed, and have come to know, that you are the Holy One of God" (vv. 68–69).

Three observations stand out to me from this incident.

First, when the narrow road narrows, many who claim to be followers of Jesus look for a broad road. "The way is hard that leads to life, and those who find it are few" (Matt. 7:14).

Second, material blessings are often more available to those who walk the broad road, who live to be blessed. And those who value physical blessings in this world more than spiritual blessings in the heavenly places will never remain on the narrow road and will therefore never fully live as feminine women or masculine men. "Blessed be the God and Father of our Lord Jesus Christ, who has blessed us in Christ with every spiritual blessing in the heavenly places" (Eph. 1:3).

Third, only the few who walk the narrow road, even as it narrows more than expected, will realize their destiny to reveal God's openness through life-inviting relational femininity or His movement through life-giving relational masculinity. "We live by believing and not by seeing . . . our goal is," not to negotiate the blessed life or to seek the healed life, but "to please him" (2 Cor. 5:7, 9 NLT).

God does His most powerful and deepest work through fully alive followers of Jesus. And because He made us male and female, it follows that the more alive women are in their God-revealing femininity and the more alive men are in their God-revealing masculinity, the more they will delight God's heart and prove useful to His purposes.

When our calling to reveal God by how we relate as gendered image-bearers is embraced as our richest act of worship, we *will* find the narrow road that leads us deeper into our calling and we *will* walk that road through life in this world no matter how narrow it gets, anchored in eternal hope, persevering in sightless faith, and irrevocably committed to sacrificial love.

Hear Jesus asking you the questions He once put to His disciples: "Will you turn away? Or will you follow Me on the narrow road? Will you believe that learning to relate as feminine women and masculine men is the way to live the life you were designed to live, the life you most want to live?"

Then listen to your converted heart respond: "Lord, what other road is there to walk? You are Life itself. Show us the way to live the life You have given us. Show us the narrow road."

25

Your Ears Shall Hear

Your ears shall hear a word behind you, saying "This is the way, walk in it."

Isaiah 30:21

Make me to know your ways, O Lord; teach me your paths.

Psalm 25:4

Teach me your way, O Lord, that I may walk in your truth.

Psalm 86:11

"For my thoughts are not your thoughts, neither are your ways my ways," declares the Lord.

Isaiah 55:8

But now let me show you a way of life that is best of all. . . . If I gave everything I have to the poor and even sacrificed my body, I could boast about it; but if I didn't love others, I would have gained nothing.

1 Corinthians 12:31; 13:3 NLT

Listen with me now to God-breathed words of Scripture, words that speak to us with thought-shifting power and life-shaping relevance. I'm listening because my thoughts have long needed shifting and my everyday relational life continually needs shaping. Why? I came into this world with an attitude.

The Way of Man

Along with everyone else born of human parents, I arrived on this planet assuming that if God existed, He existed for me. When I was told that He was a good God, it was immediately clear to me that He had no higher priority than seeing to my personal comfort. I realized, of course, that I had my part to play. If I did a reasonably good job of living by His principles and keeping most of His rules, God would be obligated by the standards of justice to pour deserved blessings into my life. That, as I understood things, was how life worked, how my life could be good.

And I also believed that I knew what made life good: a short list of things "to do today" that were easily accomplished, doctors who smiled when they looked at my test results, more money than bills, ownership in a vacation villa, kids who loved Jesus, a marriage that made me feel good about myself—the "blessed life" that I could look forward to enjoying every day. My job was to live in such a way that kept God cooperating with my plans.

Like you, I took my first step into life on the broad road. My attitude defined self-centeredness, but to me it seemed entirely reasonable, even Christian. Still today, after sixty years of claiming Jesus as my Lord, living on the broad road has its appeal.

But words from the prophet Jeremiah have been slowly shifting my thinking, and they continue to shape my relational life. Let me explain.

When Jeremiah heard that big trouble was on the horizon for God's people, the distraught prophet *confessed* something to God. When my life turns south, my impulse is to *negotiate* with God: "Lord, things aren't going so well. What can I do to get my life back on a good track?"

Jeremiah's words were different: "I know, O Lord, that the way of man is not in himself, that it is not in man who walks to direct his steps" (Jer. 10:23). In other words, "Lord, You send troubles into our lives not as problems to solve, but as opportunities to seize, opportunities for me to confess that I've been trying to lead a managed life designed to gain the satisfaction I desire, and to confess that I need You to show me the path that leads to the life I was designed to live."

When he heard that life as he knew it was about to unravel, Jeremiah confessed not only his ignorance of the ways of God but also his need for revealed wisdom from God. "Correct me, O LORD, but in justice; not in your anger, lest you bring me to nothing" (v. 24).

Never ask for God's wisdom lightly. Seeing things as they are in God's way of thinking can be difficult to handle. Remember what Solomon's search for wisdom led him to realize: "I soon discovered that God has dealt a tragic existence to the human race" (Eccles. 1:13 NLT).

Both Jeremiah and Solomon had their eyes opened to see a difficult truth: *life will not work as we want it to, and there's nothing we can do to change that reality.* Fix one problem, and another one pops up. Solve one relational conflict, and another one develops. And when God tells us how He wants us to handle ourselves in the middle of a disappointing and tension-fraught life, we're not immediately drawn to His plan. It becomes disturbingly clear that His ways do not guarantee the good life we had in mind.

When Solomon faced the reality that he could not manage his life to his satisfaction, he eventually shrugged his shoulders in weary resignation and chased after pain-numbing pleasure wherever he could find it. He became a foolish, unmasculine man. Jeremiah did something different, and became someone different.

Like Moses in the wilderness and the psalmist in distress, Jeremiah pleaded with God to show him His ways, to show him the road that would lead to life as God designed it, not to life as Jeremiah naturally envisioned it. Solomon, with all his brilliance, chose a way that *seemed* right to his intellect and instincts but proved to be dreadfully wrong. Jeremiah, in far more difficult circumstances, longed to know the way that *was* right. He wanted to walk a road through life that human wisdom would never find, that natural passions would never desire.

In his confession, Jeremiah twice used the word "man." The first use—"the way of a man is not in himself"—translates the Hebrew word *adam*, referring to the human race in general. In the second use—"it is not in man who walks to direct his steps"—"man" translates *ish*. An individual person is now in view. The point seems to be that what is true of everyone, people in general, is also true of you and me, persons in particular.

And that truth is this: no woman or man on their own, and no culture or nation with its collective religious wisdom, will ever come up with the way that God thinks.

No group of Christians and no individual Christian, without hearing from the Holy Spirit through the Book He wrote, will ever believe that a narrow road, a difficult path through a difficult world, leads to the life that every woman and man was designed to enjoy.

It's been true since Eden. It's true today. We want to believe that we can count on God to shower us with the blessings we want to enjoy in this life. Like the Israelites in Isaiah's day, we gravitate toward spiritual leaders who tell us pleasant things, lies if need be. It was no different in Paul's time. "People will not endure sound teaching, but having itching ears they will accumulate for themselves teachers to suit their own passions" (2 Tim. 4:3). And it is no different today. We resist talk of a narrow road that threatens to rob us of our freedom to live as we think best, that challenges our assumed right to have life go as we desire if we live good and moral lives.

Let me put it more starkly: it comes naturally for us to indulge a Christianized form of self-centeredness as we claim to devoutly follow Christ. Some level of self-concern seems essential to our well-being as we define it. But it is precisely that attitude, our intractable sense of feeling entitled to the "blessed life," that keeps us from falling low enough into repentance to rise high into God-revealing femininity and masculinity.

The End of Self-Centeredness

Paul's teaching is more radical than we think. Here's one example. In Philippians, he instructs us to walk a *relationally* narrow road, to live in this world, which honors self-interest as a virtue, as citizens of another world where virtue is defined differently. "Let each of you look *not only* to his own interests, *but also* to the interests of others" (Phil. 2:4; emphasis added).

Paul seems to be saying, "Look out for yourself but also look out for others." However, according to reputable Bible scholars who look carefully into the original wording, the word *only* is not there. Delete *only* and *also* is no longer needed. Paul's instruction, then, is this: "Let each of you look not to his own interests, but to the interests of others." The change in meaning is as radical as it is profound, and as profound as it is impossible—*without the Holy Spirit.*

If we are to be spiritually formed into relationally masculine men and feminine women, the *end* of self-centeredness is required, not its socialization. We are to crucify the managed life that aims toward our felt well-being. We are not to live an acceptable blend of self-centeredness and other-centeredness. There is no acceptable blend of hell's virtues with heaven's.

Jesus lived the virtue of heaven. On the dreaded cross, He made known both the holy wrath of the Father and His merciful love. In so doing He modeled and made possible an entirely new way for us to live as men and women. Rather than delivering Himself from pain, which was in His power to do, He "continued entrusting himself to him who judges justly" (1 Pet. 2:23). Perhaps no truth is more often or easily compromised in the lives of Christians than this: to be formed like Jesus means to become radically other-centered, no longer looking out for ourselves but living entirely for God and for His purposes in others.

It's true, of course, that we cannot stop desiring our own well-being. Nor should we, even if it were possible. God went to great lengths to insure our eternal wholeness and joy. But we dishonor His love when we take on the responsibility to arrange for our experience of personal well-being, to look to the good things of life and good treatment from others as the basis for our joy and meaning in this world. His call is clear. *We are to entrust our well-being to God while we live to reveal Him to others by the way we relate as men and women.*

Jeremiah's words, along with all other Spirit-inspired words, can shift our thinking and shape our way of relating. We can find our way to the narrow road when, after *conception* is followed by *conversion,* we live in *confession* by acknowledging the tragic existence of life in this world. Life will not work as we want. Before it's over, life will get difficult for all of us. We will hurt and we will fail.

 Only when we face our tragic existence as unfilled souls and imperfect lovers will we cry from our hearts, "Merciful God, forgive me. Make me to know Your ways, O Lord. Teach me Your path, that I may walk in Your truth."

As we prepare now to hear the Spirit whisper, *This is the way to living fully alive as men and women for the glory of God. Walk in it*, remember that the way is costly and the road is narrow. Remember that the word translated "narrow" in Matthew 7:14 is *thlipsis,* and that it literally means "crushing." But remember this too: God will never crush His life out of us, but He intends to crush into dust what we wrongly believe is life in order to release *His* life into the way we relate as men and women.

Listen now to God's Spirit as He reveals a way of life that is best for all of us, a path that we would never find on our own, a narrow road that is guaranteed to lead us not to the "blessed life" or the "healed life," but to the *abundant life* of fully living in true femininity or masculinity.

26

WALKING THE NARROW ROAD

The Opportunity of Defeat

Many people are surprised to learn that Christians remain subject to human passions that run contrary to God's will. They are even more surprised to learn that God can change all that; when they stumble upon this truth, it strikes them as an entirely new idea.

Dennis F. Kinlaw[1]

We are not talking here about giving up things. . . . We are talking about stripping away the craving for gratification in these things. Because it is not the things of the world that take up space in the person or do her harm. . . . The person has only *one* will, and if this gets caught up in a particular thing, it will not be free . . . yet that is what is needed if God is to transform it.

St. John of the Cross[2]

Since you have been raised to new life in Christ, set your sights on the realities of heaven.

Colossians 3:1 NLT

1. Dennis F. Kinlaw, *The Mind of Christ* (Nappanee, IN: Francis Asbury Press, 1998), 84.
2. Quoted in Iain Matthew, *The Impact of God* (London: Hodder and Stoughton, 1995), 40.

Socrates famously said that the unexamined life is not worth living. Many of us wonder, however, if the examined life is too difficult to live, especially if we let the Bible guide us in our examination. God tells us that life in this world will be filled with trouble, that we have Satan for an enemy, that we're self-deceived, and that our best deeds are stained by selfishness. It can seem too much to think about, let alone deal with. Better perhaps to focus on the more positive teachings and downplay the negatives.

But Paul had a better idea. He speaks to us in our struggles and confusion and failure and tells us to set our sights on the "realities of heaven" (Col. 3:1 NLT). He sets the pattern in Romans: face the tragic realities of earth, then look up to hear the good news. Paul is teaching us a difficult truth: *we must take a long hard look at what makes life in this world so empty and difficult before we will see how God intends to lift us up into a heavenly way to live.*

And yet we work to *not* see our tragic existence by believing two lies: one, that by our own efforts we can arrange for the blessings we want; and two, that the blessings we want have the power to provide us with the satisfaction we desire. If the blessings don't come and shattered dreams bring pain, then we scramble to find relief. The abundant life of truly living in heaven's realities as men and women remains little more than a vague ideal, a distant and perhaps unappealing dream. And even if the dream of becoming truly feminine or masculine were within reach, the road to its realization seems too hard to travel.

The Realities of Heaven

Christians who settle into a life of feeling "blessed" want to stay there. It's difficult to imagine something better than our lives going well. And when troubles do come, the longing to feel better seems all-consuming. We want at least to feel intact when things around us fall apart. As long as we set our sights no higher than on feeling good about God-blessed circumstances and God-healed emotions, we will not be able to welcome trouble and pain as opportunities from God. We will remain blind to the fact that He can use trouble and pain to release into our way of relating the femininity or masculinity He has already hardwired within our nature.

The Christian who sees life through God's eyes will *first* come face-to-face with the tragic reality that defeats every self-centered ambition *before* the liberating realities of heaven become visible, realities that will excite us with the prospect of a new way to live. But our first glimpse of the way God brings heaven's kingdom within reach is not always appealing. Shattered dreams and aching souls are the doorway through which God enters our lives, and we don't much like that idea.

The pain of lost blessings introduces us to the uncomfortable fact that we cannot and must not measure God's goodness either by the good things He provides for us in this world or by the healing protection He offers that numbs our pain when bad things happen.

When life gets hard, our natural tendency is to seek recovery or relief. It is then that selfishness is given full sway. But God has something better in mind, a *new way* to live. And He has made it available through His Son and His Spirit. Jesus told us that He came to give us the *abundant life*, not one of earthbound blessings or a satisfying experience of ourselves, but rather one of the ability to love, as men and women.

Our natural response to God's plan is to stifle a yawn as we express polite interest. Don't we all know that the Christian life centers on a God who loves us enough to give us the blessings we want and the healing we need in order to live happily in this world? It's hard to get excited about a God who enables us to love others when our lives remain difficult and we feel bad. And we never will—until we face the reality of our tragic existence that is still tragic even if we're feeling really good in a richly blessed life.

If you groan with the longing to live in God-revealing femininity or masculinity, that desire will never assume first-place priority until you face the tragic reality of your existence in this world. Until then, your priority will be to make life better or to find a way to feel better, not to cooperate with God's Spirit as He empowers you to love better. Facing reality matters, and that reality comes in two parts:

One: an inconsolable longing is lodged deep in our souls, an unquenchable desire that neither blessings nor healing can satisfy. Those who embrace this reality will feel an unendurable *emptiness* within them, an unfilled void that yearns for fullness, a void that, as they look around and within, leaves them wondering—*is this all there is?*

Two: none of us love the way we were designed to love, the way we were re-created by God's Spirit to love. We continually fall short of an ideal we can neither dismiss nor reach, yet we routinely see the failure to love in others more clearly than we see it in ourselves. Those who embrace the reality of their imperfect love will feel a sorrowful *brokenness,* a nagging sense that they miss a mark they are wrong to miss—daily. Their brokenness will not come from mistreatment *by* others but from their mistreatment *of* others.

Emptiness and brokenness: two earthbound realities we prefer to deny but must face if we're to live in heaven's realities as women and men. It seems better to live the *managed life* of living well so that life goes as planned. If life does not go well, if good results don't follow good choices, we are eager then to enter the *wounded life.* Our highest ambition becomes relief, healing from our pain, whether through escaping into an unhealthy coping activity or turning to prayer.

Socrates was right. The unexamined life is not worth living. It leaves us traveling a broad road that slowly destroys life. The unexamined life of foolishly believing that blessings and healing define the good life leads us into a dead end.

It is then, mercifully, that reality hits. Emptiness, whether we're living in blessings or troubles, and brokenness over our recognized failure to love well bring us down from the *managed life,* down through the *wounded life,* and into the *forming life* where defeat becomes a welcomed opportunity. This opportunity enables us to discover divine power to be fully alive in relational femininity or relational masculinity. It's the forming life because it is where we *want* to be formed to relate like Jesus more than we want blessings or healing.

When We're Brought Low

When the reality of emptiness and brokenness brings us low, we must wait, aware that we are unable to manage our way to satisfaction through the blessings available in this world and unable to heal our wounds in a deep, lasting way that frees us to love as men and women. As we sink into the depths of distress and defeat, we are confronted with only two options: *give up on life* or *seek God for life.* Our misery becomes an agonizing opportunity to "earnestly seek" God (Hos. 5:15).

Seek Him, for what? For the recovery of the "blessed life"? No. Blessings have been exposed as unsatisfying. We're now aiming higher. For relief in the "healed life"? No again. A good self-image now means little while we continue to love poorly.

In the emptiness of inconsolable longing and in the brokenness of never loving without the stain of self-interest, we are released to seek God for one thing: *to know Him as our forgiving and empowering Father.* From the dark depths of despair we look up, crying out to catch a glimpse of the bright reality of heaven. We risk, hoping that we could somehow delight in God's unexplainable delight in us, and that by the way we relate we could pass His delight on to others.

The emptiness we feel and the brokenness we own creates space within us that eagerly, even desperately, waits for God and for nothing and no one less. As St. John of the Cross put it, our misery strips away the "craving for gratification" in the blessings of life or the healing of pain.

So we wait. We pray. We wake up at two in the morning, troubled, unable to sleep. We read our Bibles, sometimes comforted, sometimes confused, sometimes convicted. We worship, moved to tears of joy or feeling dry as a bone. We seek spiritual community. A friend touches our heart. Another misses us.

We wait, demanding nothing, surrendering everything. Our hope is in Christ alone. We confess our tragic reality as we wait to be caught up in His beautiful reality.

—

As I write these words, I am six weeks past my sixty-eighth birthday. I was born in the summer of 1944. I was converted eight summers later. In the six decades since I was born into God's family, I have known dark nights and bright mornings. The darkness of God's felt absence when I was in turmoil sometimes made me wonder if I really had been converted. The brightness of God's felt presence, experienced mostly when the Bible came alive for me, brought me a too brief but very real taste of inexpressible joy.

Only recently have I caught what I believe is a clear glimpse of what God had in mind when He formed me as a male. I am increasingly sustained, sometimes invigorated, by what it means for the realities of heaven to form me into a masculine man, fully alive for the glory of God. However, the clearer the vision develops of what I could be, the more clearly I realize what I have not yet become.

I am beginning to enjoy the fruit of confession in a new way. More frequently and with greater intensity I now experience the reality of emptiness and brokenness, at a depth I have not before known, and I seem to be embracing this reality more willingly, even gratefully, without a fight, and with results I have long been waiting for.

It is the supernatural result of embracing the tragic reality of emptiness and brokenness that I now want to make known. Words, of course, fail me. I neither want to overstate nor understate what is happening in me, and what is happening or could happen in you.

I am more tempted to emphasize what is not yet happening, to focus on me, on my ongoing struggles and failure. I am very aware that the joy of being *fully* alive as a man will not be mine till heaven. But I am increasingly aware that what is available now is deeply good. It's my *life*.

No human language can capture the mystery of what God's Spirit can do in an empty and broken heart. But a strange confidence develops: the deeper I sink into the darkness of my *self*, the higher I can rise into the light of Christ that will then fill my soul and be revealed in the way I relate. In that confidence, I am discovering a quiet rest beneath my noisy angst. In that hope I am tasting freedom, the freedom to move toward others in any circumstance of life and in any condition of soul.

27

BECOMING MASCULINE MEN AND FEMININE WOMEN

The church . . . is a communion created by Christ and founded upon him, one in which Christ reveals himself . . . as the new humanity itself.

Dietrich Bonhoeffer[1]

The fullness of being human . . . lies not only in the male or only in the female but in the communion of male and female.

Mauro Meruzzi[2]

Let me now complete this book by summarizing the process by which God's Spirit forms Christian women into feminine women and Christian men into masculine men who can meet on the Bridge of Connection. The process is the same for both women and men. The outcome is wonderfully unique.

Confession

Confession embraces defeat as an opportunity to walk the narrow road to life.

1. Charles Ringma, *Seize the Day with Dietrich Bonhoeffer* (Colorado Springs, CO: Pinon Press, 2000), October 26.
2. Mauro Meruzzi, "Woman and her complementary relationship to man," *Contending Modernities*, November 1, 2012, http://blogs.nd.edu/contendingmodernities2012/11/01.

The reality of our tragic existence is deeply felt.

When the Spirit begins His deep work, we feel desperate in our empti-ness, which we can neither fill nor ignore. And, thanks to Him, we own our relational shortcomings as sin, leaving us broken, suffering from our inability to love others as Christ loves us.

We embrace the tragic reality of our emptiness and brokenness.

We cease fighting the truth of what we're now experiencing, no longer treating our sorrow and failure as an enemy to defeat, realizing instead that this difficult reality is an opportunity to accept our defeat and thus make room for God's transforming power.

We wait.

We pray not to negotiate but to surrender. We hope, more intently, for neither superficial blessings nor pleasant feelings but for the release of the abundant life, for growth in our God-provided ability to love.

We discern evidence of the Spirit's working.

Unendurable emptiness slowly changes into hopeful thirst. We identify with the psalmist: "One thing have I asked of the LORD, that will I seek after" (Ps. 27:4). Though still strong, our longing for blessings and healing takes a backseat to a non-pressured desire, "that I may dwell in the house of the LORD all the days of my life, to gaze upon the beauty of the LORD" (Ps. 27:4). Our thirst to know God awakens us to our ultimate desire: "Come, Lord Jesus" (Rev. 22:20). It is no accident that reading God's love letters leaves us wanting nothing more than to go home to be with Jesus, to see Him and to dance forever in perfect rhythm with the Trinity when we join the Eternal Party of Love.

We discern the Spirit's further work.

The more we long to dance with the Trinity by loving like Jesus, the more we recognize that our best moves are not yet in perfect rhythm with the Spirit. Brokenness deepens, not into self-contempt but into exhila-rating gratitude to God. Forgiven? For every relational failure? Amazing love, how can it be! The agony of brokenness becomes a celebration of grace. Only those broken by relational failure can hear the sweet music of divine love.

Hope becomes the solid foundation on which we can build a new way to relate.

As emptiness becomes thirst and brokenness becomes gratitude, hope stirs with life. We continue to hurt, struggle, and fail. But our hope remains firm. The One who began a good work at our conversion is deepening that work through our confession, and He will "bring it to completion at the day of Jesus Christ" (Phil. 1:6). The journey unfolds: conception to conversion, conversion to confession, confession to completion. Every empty heart will be fully satisfied in God. Every broken soul will be empowered to love like Jesus. Our sure hope sustains us.

The anchor of hope strengthens our faith.

Paul thanked God that "because of the hope laid up" for the Colossian Christians in heaven, they were now firmly grounded in faith (see Col. 1:4–5). A lesson is learned: faith survives doubt when hope is alive; more, faith thrives. No dark night can destroy our hope-supported faith that God is doing us good. We live with confident hope that morning will come. It may be Friday, but Sunday's coming!

Faith strengthened by hope releases love.

The battle continues. Evil flesh is still with us. Women are tempted to self-protectively close up when danger threatens. Men want to self-protectively back off when failure seems imminent. But our experience of emptiness and brokenness has weakened both our demand to get all that we want from life and our efforts to control or deny the realistic fear that bad things can happen. As we die to the demand for fair treatment from others, we come alive with the desire to reveal God to those who hurt us. We may hurt, but we can love. Our hope for a better day and our faith that it's coming free us to love now. When our duty to love becomes our desire and delight, it is then that divine love energizes the way we relate.

It is then that we taste the abundant life.

Blessings may continue, lost blessings may be restored—or they may not. We may experience the healing presence of God—or we may not. But in any circumstance of life or in any condition of soul, we become aware of an abundance of the desire and the power to love. We may not feel them, but we somehow know that both are there, alive within us. We *want* to love. We *can* love. And sometimes we do just that. We love!

Then something happens, and we must cycle through the process again.

Perhaps it's pride, the illusion that we've arrived. Maybe another dream shatters or long-buried pain resurfaces. It could be mounting pressure or the resurgence of a powerful addiction. We find ourselves longing for restored blessings or healing peace. We try to do right. We live for relief. And then the Spirit, who never gives up on us, grants us another glimpse of reality, this one deeper, more unsettling. The experience of emptiness and brokenness returns. Behind us, we hear a gentle voice reminding us, "This is the way, walk in it" (Isa. 30:21). With thirsty and grateful hearts, we remember that Christ is in us, "the hope of glory" (Col. 1:27). Faith is again strengthened, the longing to love again burns within us, and we resume our journey on the narrow road. We enter another season of living the abundant life. And prayer rises from our renewed hearts: "A longer season, Lord, deeper and richer this time, until a season of abundant life becomes an eternity of joy. Come, Lord Jesus!"

Abundant Life

When a woman walks the narrow road to the abundant life, she becomes alive in femininity.

Without trying to be feminine, it happens. She loves as a woman because God made her a woman. She is opened to receive and eager to nourish. She discovers the joy of living in relational femininity, not through strenuous effort but through glad surrender to the Spirit's heavenly wisdom, leading, and power.

When a man walks the narrow road to the abundant life, he becomes alive in masculinity.

Without trying to be masculine, it happens. He loves as a man because God made him a man. He bends his ear close to another's heart to hear their groaning, and then he moves into relationships with life-giving love. He discovers the joy of living in relational masculinity, not through strenuous effort but through glad surrender to the Spirit's heavenly wisdom, leading, and power.

The man and woman meet on the bridge. She invites. He moves. Or two women meet in the mutual enjoyment of their femininity, or two men meet in the mutual enjoyment of their masculinity. The reality of heaven, the kingdom of God, comes to earth, visible in the community of feminine women and masculine men. May it be.

Epilogue

A Final Word to Women and Men

To Women

If you experience same-sex attraction; if you struggle with body image concerns and eating disorders; if you relieve pain in your soul by cutting your body or filling your emptiness with sex, drugs, alcohol, or suicide attempts: **you remain a woman.**

If you feel insecure about your appearance or ashamed of your weaknesses, if you've been sexually or emotionally abused and live with hatred and fear, if you were raised in a family with parents and siblings who never *saw* you: **nothing changes the fact that you are a woman.**

If you're a teenage girl enduring problems you've shared with no one, if you're single and wondering why you're not married or married and wishing you were single, if you're fighting to make your way as a woman in a man's world: **your core identity is woman.**

If you're attractive and healthy; if you're a respected lawyer, pastor, medical professional, businesswoman, or teacher; if you function well in relationships and responsibilities as a wife and mother or as an active and fulfilled single: **claim your highest privilege to relate as a woman.**

DON'T label yourself by your struggles and symptoms.

DON'T define yourself by your history and emotions.

DON'T identify yourself by your circumstances and challenges.
DON'T limit yourself by your success and satisfaction.

Hear God's call to come alive in relational femininity!

An authentically feminine woman is a woman so at rest in God's delight in her indestructible beauty that she refuses to be a slave to her fear of invisibility. She therefore invites others to enjoy the beauty of the God whose love casts out the power of fear as she relates:

- invitationally, not controllingly
- openly, not guardedly
- courageously, not defensively
- freely, not protectively

She relates with one embraced purpose in mind: to encourage others to be consumed and transformed by the beauty of the God who sees, invites, nourishes, and enjoys His people.

To Men

If you feel homosexual desire; if the pleasure of pornography seems irresistible; if you numb your pain with sex, drugs, alcohol, or a more subtle addiction such as humor, sarcasm, or aggression: **you remain a man.**

If you feel inadequate to make the difference you want to make and therefore struggle with a sense of insignificance, if you experienced devastating abuse in your family or during your days in school, if you were raised by a dad who either pushed or neglected you or by a mother who criticized or overprotected you: **nothing changes the fact that you are a man.**

If you're a teenage boy with private struggles or shameful secrets, if you're single and wondering why you're not married or married and wishing you were single, if you're fighting to measure up as a man in a man's world: **your core identity is man.**

If you're healthy and in good shape; if you're successful as a leader in church, business, or politics; if you function well in relationships and responsibilities as a husband and dad, with business colleagues or sports buddies, or as a productively active single: **claim your highest privilege to relate as a man.**

DON'T label yourself by your struggles and symptoms.
DON'T define yourself by your history and emotions.
DON'T identify yourself by your circumstances and challenges.
DON'T limit yourself by your success and satisfaction.

Hear God's call to come alive in relational masculinity!

An authentically masculine man is a man so grateful for his call to move toward others with the weight of divine impact that he confronts his paralyzing fear of weightlessness by relating in order to:

- hear the struggles of another
- remember his privileged opportunity to move toward another and to do for another whatever he discerns will reveal the nature of the God who sees the worst in another, feels its impact on Him, and yet refuses to back away
- explore the depths of that struggle until he is aware of no stronger ambition than to be with another in unthreatening presence
- sacrifice himself for the pleasure of serving the needs of another

He relates with one embraced purpose in mind: to encourage others to trust and to rest in the beauty of the God who is always moving toward others in love.

Women offer a glimpse of heaven's beauty. They display God's invitation to draw near to Him. Men present a look into heaven's beauty as well as they show God's movement toward us that reveals His love.

The vision has been cast. We may not change the world, but we can put God on display in our world. Make the difference you were designed to make in other people's lives by revealing the irresistible beauty of God as you relate like Jesus in the Spirit's power.

May we all live to reveal the God we love, as feminine women and masculine men.

Afterword

As an increasingly fully alive woman, I want to add my voice to what I believe is an important and liberating book. A brief history might help to communicate what is most alive in me as I reflect on what Larry has written.

As I write these words, Larry and I are nearing our forty-seventh anniversary. We met at age ten, had our first "date" at twelve, married just a few weeks short of twenty-two, and have known each other now for fifty-eight of the sixty-eight years since our births. A look back at our growing-up years makes it clear to both of us that we've been on a long, slow journey toward understanding what it means to be fully alive as a man and woman for the glory of God.

Our parents were deeply committed Christians who followed what they believed was God's call on their lives. Our fathers understood their "role" as men to provide for their families as the primary breadwinner (a traditional term I often heard as a child) and to assume responsibility for spiritual leadership. Our mothers accepted their "role" to submissively follow their husband's lead and to quietly do their part as supportive helpmeets.

Neither Larry nor I have any doubt that our parents loved each other as faithful spouses and that they lived their understanding of what it meant to follow Christ. We do, however, wonder whether their declared belief in God as a Trinity of three divine Persons made them aware that they were called to reveal God uniquely by how they related as men and women. It saddens us to think that our parents did not appear to think about what it would mean to be fully alive as image-bearing male and female.

With little or no teaching or modeling on Trinitarian relating in my background, I am grateful to now have a vision of living alive as an opened woman. Every day I face the reality of relational sin, of closing my feminine soul to others to protect myself from hurt, a core terror that took shape in me at age eight, when abuse from a neighbor began. But every day I more clearly feel the delight of living as the God-revealing woman I was redeemed to become.

Submissive? Yes! Gentle and quiet? Of course! A suitable helper to my husband? A privilege! But in a new way that frees me to live beyond stereo-types, to increasingly be all that I am as a feminine bearer of God's image.

Thanks to the message of *Fully Alive* I can look forward to my senior years knowing that the true beauty of my womanhood will never fade but only deepen. God has used Larry's teaching in this book to awaken me to taste the freedom to live for God's glory as a relationally feminine woman. Larry lives the message of his book too, and I have been the joyful recipient of a husband who moves toward me and toward God, living in relational masculinity. We meet on the bridge.

Whether you're married or single, old or young, enjoying a blessed life or struggling through difficulties, I pray that *Fully Alive* will awaken you to the privilege of revealing our relational God by relating as a feminine woman or masculine man.

Glory to God!

Rachael Crabb

Fully Alive together
for nearly fifty years.

Dr. Larry Crabb is a well-known psychologist, conference and seminar speaker, Bible teacher, popular author, and founder/director of NewWay Ministries. In addition to various other speaking and teaching opportunities, Dr. Crabb offers several weekend conferences throughout the country and a weeklong School of Spiritual Direction held in Colorado Springs, CO, or Asheville, NC. He is currently Scholar in Residence at Colorado Christian University in Colorado, and Visiting Professor for Richmont Graduate University in Georgia. Dr. Crabb has authored many books, including *Inside Out*, *Understanding People*, *The Marriage Builder*, *Finding God*, *Connecting*, *Becoming a True Spiritual Community*, *The Pressure's Off*, *Shattered Dreams*, *SoulTalk*, *The SoulCare Experience DVD*, *The PAPA Prayer*, *Real Church*, and *66 Love Letters*. Dr. Crabb and his wife, Rachael, live in the Denver area.

For additional information, please visit www.newwayministries.org.

New Way MINISTRIES

NEWWAY MINISTRIES WAS FORMED IN 2002 BY DR. LARRY CRABB.

It was birthed out of the passionate conviction that there is a new way to live made possible by the New Covenant that must become better known. We seek to introduce people to this new way of living, thinking, and relating that only the gospel makes possible. Our intended contribution to this revolution occurs through four distinct ministries:

- *Conferences*
- *School of Spiritual Direction*
- *Resource Library*
- *Internet Courses and Certification*

Dr. Crabb's work focuses on a biblical understanding of various aspects of life, such as marriage and manhood. Today, Larry is zeroing in on three topics:

- *Encounter*—what it means to experience God
- *Transformation*—what it takes to become like Christ
- *Community*—what real community is and how it helps us experience God and become spiritually formed

DR. LARRY CRABB is a psychologist, speaker, Bible teacher, bestselling author, and founder/director of **NewWay Ministries**

Our Calling - To ignite a revolution in relationships, a new way to live that explores the real battle in our souls and frees us to value intimacy with God more than blessings from God. It's a new way that's as old as the Bible. It's what following Jesus is all about.

Our Mission - To equip followers of Jesus to *enter the battle* for the souls of those they love—the battle to resist the Old Way and live the New Way.

www.newwayministries.org
info@newwayministries.org
phone: 970.262.9110
fax: 970.468.9696